Turbulent Times

Turbulent Times

THE MEMOIRS OF

RONALD McINTOSH

First published in Great Britain in 2014 by
Biteback Publishing Ltd
Westminster Tower
3 Albert Embankment
London SE1 7SP

ISBN 978-1-84954-804-5

10 9 8 7 6 5 4 3 2 1

A CIP catalogue record for this book is available from the British Library.

Set in Adobe Garamond Pro by five-twentyfive.com

Printed and bound in Great Britain by
CPI Group (UK) Ltd, Croydon CR0 4YY

In loving, grateful memory of Doreen, Chrissie and Tom

CONTENTS

–FOREWORD–

PETER HENNESSY

RONNIE MCINTOSH WAS a member of what his friend and Whitehall colleague, Ian Bancroft, called 'the generation for whom everything was possible'; the young men and (rather fewer) young women who had returned from war service to join a civil service tasked by the Attlee government to build a better economy and society out of the rubble of a total war – a Britain that would never again return to the unemployment, poverty and sheer waste of human lives and talents that had characterised so many of the inter-war years.

Maynard Keynes had given them the techniques to engineer and sustain full employment. William Beveridge had given them the blueprint for a healthier, better educated, more fulfilled and productive British people. It was the task of Ronnie's generation of officials to help set the country on a virtuous circle of prosperity and social justice.

This is much more than a fascinating autobiography. It is part of the story of how that generation and the country fared. Ronnie found himself at various stages near or close to the epicentres of power culminating in his leadership of the National Economic Development Office (Neddy) as the ingredients of that shining post-war settlement – and the high level of political consensus that went with it – began to tarnish and then to crack in the 1970s.

Ronnie has never lost sight of the ideas and ideals or the high sense of public service of his formative years. He is also a realist. He knows just how difficult it has been in the UK to fuse liberal capitalism (the best engine of growth and innovation so far known to man) with social democracy (the most effective way of mitigating capitalism's harshness and sustaining a fair and settled society). You read his chapters and you are in the hands of a sensitive and highly knowledgeable guide to the achievements and the vicissitudes of Britain since 1945.

There are several bonuses in this book. Pre-war Oxford. Wartime service in the Merchant marine. A portrait of a very happy marriage. The story of developing and flourishing religious views. An additional bonus is Ronnie's financial and industrial life after leaving the public service, in the City and especially in the new Russia emerging from the ruins of the Cold War. Those who don't know him will come to appreciate why those who do cherish so highly Ronnie's friendship and wisdom.

PETER HENNESSY, FBA
ATTLEE PROFESSOR OF CONTEMPORARY BRITISH HISTORY,
QUEEN MARY, UNIVERSITY OF LONDON

-CHAPTER ONE-

CHARTERHOUSE

ONE OF THE best things to happen to me in my formative years was that I failed the Winchester scholarship. My father had rather wanted me to go to Stowe, the public school founded four years after I was born, whose headmaster J. F. Roxburgh was a visionary figure with a high reputation. Like all my relatives on both sides of the family, my father was Scottish-born: my sister and I were the first members of my extended family to be born south of the border (in my case not very far south, in Cumbria) – much to the disapproval of our older relatives. My father didn't know a great deal about the English public schools but believed – perhaps correctly – that the Scottish system was far superior. He himself had been at Dollar Academy, a school with a fine academic record to which boys with the requisite ability and promise were admitted regardless of their parents' income.

For this reason he relied heavily on my prep school headmaster, Percy Linford, for advice on what school I should go on to when the time came. Linford was a larger than

life figure – a gifted teacher, with a limp that was said to be the result of falling off a sledge on the way from Moscow to Saint Petersburg before the First World War. He was the proprietor as well as the headmaster of his school and very ambitious for it, and he thought I had a chance of getting a Winchester scholarship, which would be a good advertisement for the school. So, early in 1933, when I was approaching my fourteenth birthday, I set off to Winchester to take the exam, in company with one of my prep school contemporaries, Lawrence Stone. We both failed.

In retrospect, Stone's failure is more surprising than mine. He was an extremely clever boy with an original mind and later made a name for himself as a historian by having an article published in one of the learned journals which he had written, without access to any library, on board his Royal Navy ship during the war. His subsequent career as a lecturer and fellow of Wadham College, Oxford was startling. Following the publication of a paper he wrote on the Elizabethan aristocracy, the then Professor of Economic History opined that 'in ten years' time no economic historian in England will be able to hold a candle to Stone'. A few years later, after serious errors were said to have been found in a subsequent paper, Hugh Trevor-Roper, the future Regius Professor of History and never one to be shy of criticising his peers, wrote that 'Stone is in my opinion (and now, I think, in everyone's opinion) a charlatan'. Before very long Stone departed for Princeton, where in due course he became Dodge Professor of History and gained a high reputation for his ebullient style of lecturing and innovative approach to social history. Whatever the rights and wrongs of the Oxford controversy, I would have expected the fourteen-year-old Stone to sail through the Winchester exam.

My own position was different. No doubt I had a lively mind and my intellectual interests were already quite wide, but I have never thought of myself as having a scholarly bent nor have I been interested in erudition for its own sake. So I cannot fault the examiners' judgement in my case – and I have never regretted their decision.

Shortly after our failure at Winchester, Stone and I took the Charterhouse exam and were both awarded scholarships; to my surprise and pleasure I came out joint top of the list. Charterhouse, founded in 1611 and translated in the 1870s to a spectacular hilltop site near Godalming, was in fact much more suitable for me than Winchester. The story of three public school boys in which the Wykehamist points out that a young lady near them seems to want a chair, the Harrovian fetches one and the Carthusian sits on it, is no doubt apocryphal but it perhaps illustrates my old school's aptitude for producing young men of a practical disposition.

In my time the pupils were of course all male and came from a mix of backgrounds; many of their fathers were army officers, stockbrokers, doctors (like mine) and clergymen but few, if any, owned a grouse moor. My contemporaries were a lively bunch of varied provenance. Two very good friends of mine, who at this distance stand out most clearly in my memory, were from contrasting backgrounds. Peston Ginwala, the top scholar in the year ahead of me, was the son of a well-off family of Calcutta Parsees and had an intellect of a quality I have otherwise encountered only in Isaiah Berlin. Ginwala was a delightful, rather gentle boy, who was very well liked and respected by his peers; I remember him telling me that he never encountered any references – let alone critical ones – to the colour of his skin at school and became aware that it could cause problems only after he had left. In 1937 he went on to Oxford, where he would undoubtedly have achieved high academic honours: but on the outbreak of war he returned to India, became a successful lawyer and, to my astonishment, a pillar of the Royal Calcutta Turf Club and sadly I never saw him again.

Ronnie Millar, my exact contemporary and also a scholar, was brought up by his single mother (his father having died when he was four) who took to the stage to pay for her son's education and by the time I got to know Ronnie had become the leading lady in a well-known theatrical touring company. Ronnie was a hugely entertaining man who had the theatre in his blood; he became a successful playwright, notable in particular for his dramatisations of several of C. P. Snow's novels.[1] Later on, he became Margaret

1 He also wrote an engaging memoir, *A View from the Wings* (Weidenfeld & Nicolson; London, 1993)

Thatcher's speechwriter and provided her with one of her most memorable lines: 'You turn if you want to – the lady's not for turning.' Ronnie was knighted in 1980 and at his memorial service in the Actors' Church in Covent Garden in 1998 two former Prime Ministers (Thatcher and John Major) read the lessons.

Many people looking back on their schooldays remember a single person whose inspirational teaching opened the door for them to a lifelong interest in a particular subject – drama, poetry, biology or whatever. For Ginwala, Millar and me this person was A. L. ('Uncle') Irvine who taught classics to the sixth form. Irvine was a rather nondescript-looking, unassuming man who wrote in his memoirs: 'I began as a second rate scholar and ended as one: but I also began and ended as an enthusiast. The one real qualification I could claim as a teacher was the power of enjoyment.'[2] It wasn't his teaching of classics that inspired me. I am grateful for my classical education, which made me understand the connection between the use of language and clear thinking, but in retrospect I consider that boys at the old public schools spent too much time on Latin and Greek (my father thought the same and paid for me to have private tuition in German).

The enthusiasm which Irvine imparted was his wholehearted but discriminating love of English literature. He did this by reserving an hour every Tuesday afternoon for

2 *Sixty Years at School* (P&G Wells Ltd; Winchester, 1958)

reading aloud to us carefully chosen pieces of English writing which we might not yet have come across – and, as he wrote, 'occasionally at other times setting Demosthenes or Tacitus aside for an hour while I read aloud the trial of Mr Pickwick'. This was how I first became aware, for example, of Dr Johnson, Trollope and the poet A. E. Housman, all of whom in later life I have found a lot more rewarding than Cicero (whom, like many academics of his day, Irvine called 'Tully').

The outstanding personality of the Charterhouse in which I grew up was, however, Robert Birley. In my first two years the headmaster was Sir Frank Fletcher, a mild, scholarly man who had a high reputation in and beyond the school. But at sixty-four he was too remote a figure to be of much interest to a fourteen-year-old boy. At thirty-one, Birley, who succeeded him, was the youngest man ever to be appointed head of a major public school and his effect on us teenagers was electric. A tall, gangly and unathletic figure, he broke the mould not only with his youthfulness but because he was a historian rather than a classicist. He was also a devout Christian and a man of strong liberal principles, as his subsequent work in post-war Germany and apartheid South Africa plainly showed; and though his political views would now be considered only mildly left of centre, they were enough for him to acquire in the 1930s the nickname of 'Red Robert'. For me, his arrival when I was just sixteen was a breath of fresh air and his influence on my developing views on life, society, culture and other great issues which concern an adolescent as he grows into maturity, was substantial.

After twelve years at Charterhouse, Birley (who later became headmaster of Eton) was appointed to lead the effort to rebuild and transform the education system in the western zone of occupied Germany, with the aim of creating a democratic country out of the devastation that accompanied Hitler's defeat. As a fairly frequent visitor to Germany over the years, I have become a great admirer of the way in which its post-war citizens have come to terms with their past, and of their determination to play a constructive part in the European comity of nations. Birley and his colleagues in the Education Department clearly made a significant contribution to this process in the early post-war years.

In 1950 Birley helped Frau Lilo Milchsack, whose husband had been a prominent anti-Nazi mayor of Leipzig, to found the Königswinter conferences. These brought together politicians, journalists and other opinion-formers from Germany and Britain to hold joint discussions in a relaxed atmosphere, and played a constructive part in the process of post-war reconciliation. At Shirley Williams's[3] suggestion, I was invited to some of these conferences in the 1970s and saw the huge respect in which the 75-year-old Birley was still held by leading Germans.

---

3 Labour Cabinet minister (1974–79) and one of the founders of the Social Democratic Party (SDP). Now Baroness Williams of Crosby

I thoroughly enjoyed my time at Charterhouse, which played a big part in making me the person I became in my maturity. I was made head of my house (always called Duckites because its nineteenth-century founder Dr Girdlestone waddled like a duck) in 1936; and I look back with some pride on the decision my fellow monitors (prefects) and I took to abolish corporal punishment, which we were at the time entitled to inflict on errant juniors, in our domain. A year later I was appointed head of the school by Robert Birley, which made me think even more highly of him – and gave me an unforgettable experience when, as a seventeen-year-old, I had to read the lesson at the open air service held to mark the laying of the foundation stone of Guildford Cathedral in 1937.

I was never a great ball-player – skiing, swimming and sailing have been my preferred sporting activities – but I scraped into the school team for hockey, which we played in the post-Christmas term. In February 1938 the team travelled to Germany to play a team of our own age in Munich. The eleven young Germans who spent the first evening with us, drinking copious quantities of Munich's famous product, seemed a decent group, with no overt signs of Nazism, and we had a pleasant time together. But as we made our way on to the pitch somewhat blearily the next day, we were dismayed to find that the eleven Germans facing us were not the youngsters we had met the previous evening but a quite different group, fresh in wind and limb. I am afraid I no longer remember the result of the match but I feel sure we didn't win.

With all this to look back on it grieves me to raise a question about the justification at the present time for schools like Charterhouse and the role they play in our present day society. At the time we were there, my fellow schoolboys and I were very conscious of the privileged life we were leading: in retrospect, the degree of privilege that I and others like me enjoyed at school and university seems grotesque. If we had been told that public schools like ours would still be in existence, more or less unchanged, in the twenty-first century, we would have laughed aloud in disbelief – and thought that the idea was in any case not only absurd but undesirable.

We were clearly not alone in this. As early as 1942, when the end of the war was not yet in sight, the government appointed a high-powered committee to look into the relationship between the public schools and the state education system. Birley was a member of the committee and played a key part in writing its report,[4] which was published in 1944, the year R. A. Butler's landmark Education Act was enacted. I can clearly remember the impact the report

4 *The Fleming Report: The Public Schools and the General Education System* (HMSO; London, 1944)

made on those of us who were interested in the subject and the public discussion that followed. The report itself was not particularly radical – it didn't call for the abolition of public schools, which quite a lot of people were advocating at the time, but it did say quite definitely that educational choices should not depend on financial considerations, and proposed a series of reforms, under which local authorities would fund public school education for those who qualified but were unable to afford the fees.

Birley's view was clear. He believed that public schools should come to terms with the state 'not merely from the point of view of the survival of the public schools but rather of what they could contribute to the nation; the onus was on them to take the initiative with bold and sensible experiments'. But sadly, the report's recommendations led to nothing. Some local authorities tried to make a success of them but the initial momentum petered out when other calls on expenditure proved more pressing. A great opportunity was missed.

In those days men who had been to public schools almost always wore their old school ties, which identified them in the way a pair of Adidas trainers might identify a less privileged youngster today. Groucho Marx parodied this in one of his films, when on meeting a man for the first time he pointed to his tie and said, 'I see you were at Harrods: what house were you in?' Old school ties are rarely worn nowadays but the public schools still exist as providers of privilege and definers of social class; and the division between them and secondary schools in the state sector is, if anything, greater than it was when I was young.

Public schools have brought many benefits not just by the quality of the education they give their pupils but to the country as a whole – when Britain had an empire it was very largely run by ex-public school boys, who by and large did a good job. But there has been a big downside. These same schools have been a major influence in perpetuating the existence of the 'two nation' society which, in my opinion, has diminished Britain for more than a century. It is a huge disappointment to me that, despite constructive initiatives from Wellington, Eton and Westminster, the public schools have not been able to summon the collective will to share their skills and experience with the state sector, as a matter of course and on the scale needed to bring lasting change.

Governing bodies and heads are, of course, aware of the problem: but many of them seem so preoccupied with the need to attract Chinese, Russian and other foreign boys and girls to their schools, and so concerned that those they now call their 'competitors' may do better than them at this, that they appear to shut their eyes to the inherent dangers to society in the present situation.

Happily, the new headmaster of my old school, Richard Pleming, who took up his post in January 2014, is a man after my own heart and we are on the same wavelength on this subject. Pleming is determined that Charterhouse should become one of the leaders in tackling the problems of social disadvantage and inequality in education and that active engagement in this field should, in his words, 'lie at the heart of the school's mission and be woven into the DNA of all it does'. To help him to achieve this ambition – for which I understand he has the governing body's strong support – he proposes to create a new post of Director of Social Responsibility at the school. My personal view is that the top priority for independent schools in this field should now be helping state schools to raise their game. Charterhouse already has a toe in the water in this respect through a unique residential summer programme it runs for state school physics and chemistry teachers and I hope that the new initiative may enable it to undertake this type of work on a much larger scale. It has, therefore, been a real pleasure for me to become the first Old Carthusian to pledge financial support for the headmaster's plan for the school to take its rightful place among the leaders in this field.

–CHAPTER TWO–

IN THE SHADOW OF THE GREAT WAR

BORN IN SEPTEMBER 1919, I must have been conceived, give or take a week or two, around Armistice night 1918. My childhood was, as a result, dominated by the First World War, to which grown-up conversation, public ceremonies, plays, poetry and books constantly returned. To a considerable extent my attitude to life and my deepest convictions were moulded by this.

The effect was to make me an out-and-out pacifist from the start of my thinking life; and although I abandoned my pacifism in 1940, abhorrence of war in all its forms has remained a central part of my character. Rightly or wrongly, I believe that we were born into the world for a purpose and that purpose was not to kill one another.

This attitude was not uncommon among my contemporaries. We were the generation whose elder brothers resolved in an Oxford Union debate in 1933 that they would never fight for king and country. Subsequent generations – their views shaped by later historical events – have found it hard to understand how a group of privileged young men could take such a position. But I remember as clearly as if it were yesterday that, as schoolboys, my classmates and I were determined that, whatever mistakes we might make when we grew up, we would not in any circumstances repeat the human catastrophes of Passchendaele and Verdun.

Almost everyone I knew at school had lost a relative in that war – in my case my uncle Rae was killed in 1915, assaulting a famous place near Ypres called simply 'Hill 62'. At Charterhouse the cathedral-like school chapel we attended every day was built to honour – and was big enough to have accommodated – the nearly 700 Old Carthusians killed in the war. So, as we watched R. C. Sherriff's *Journey's End*, read Robert Graves's *Goodbye to All That*, Vera Brittain's *Testament of Youth* and Siegfried Sassoon's *Memoirs of an Infantry Officer* and were bowled over by Wilfred Owen's poem 'Dulce et decorum est pro patria mori' (written barely a year before he did just that in 1918) we were resolved that we would plot a different course through life from the one taken by our fathers' generation – and would eschew not only militarism but nationalism, which was widely held by our history teachers and others to have been the root cause of the war.

The rise of Hitler, the Spanish Civil War and Mussolini's invasion of Abyssinia seemed to many people to make the pacifist case unconvincing: but the 1930s were also the decade of the Peace Pledge Union and my pacifist faith remained intact. I had, however, a natural desire to share the dangers to which my non-pacifist peers would be exposed if war broke out and so, when the time came, I decided to join the Merchant Navy before I was called up. Within less than two months after the outbreak of war I went to sea as a cadet. When I ceased to be a pacifist in 1940, I considered applying for a transfer to the Royal Navy, but on reflection there seemed no real point in doing so. I thought that, as by then a merchant seaman of some experience, I would probably be of more use staying where I was and I think the authorities would have shared this view. So I continued in the Merchant Navy until the end of 1945, when I returned to Oxford to complete my degree.

After the war I did not revert to my youthful pacifism – though I retain my abhorrence of war, as I think all decent human beings should. I now believe that Britain should maintain a naval, military and air capability of a size appropriate to a medium-sized island nation with a long democratic history but limited resources; and I favour keeping our nuclear deterrent in the form of Trident or whatever succeeds it.

I do not, however, believe that we should aim to 'punch above our weight'. I regard this as a pernicious (and almost by definition self-defeating) doctrine introduced in a moment of aberration by the former Foreign Secretary Douglas Hurd, whom I have otherwise admired since I first met him, as Ted Heath's political secretary, in 1970. I was shocked to see that in 2014 a senior general referred to the ability to punch above our weight as the yardstick by which the Ministry of Defence still measures itself.[5]

Britain has spent a large part of my adult lifetime struggling to adjust psychologically to the loss of its empire and its great power status in the world. I have been surprised at how difficult some of the post-imperial generation of politicians and commentators seem to find this. For me – and I think for most of my generation, which grew up in a world where the sun never set on the British Empire – the policy of granting independence to our overseas possessions, which successive governments have followed since 1947, has been inevitable, realistic and morally right. I take pride in the fact that in my lifetime we have, by and large, surrendered our large empire peacefully and with reasonable grace – the loss of empire should not be considered a matter for nostalgia or regret but a sign of our maturity and, perhaps one can say, decency; and for the generation which lived through 1939–45, the consequent change in Britain's position in the world has not been difficult to accept. But the British seem to have an inbred desire to tell other people how to run their lives and it has been sad to see how in recent years our young, Manichean political leaders have clung to this

5 General Sir Richard Sherriff, *Sunday Times*, 30 March 2014

unattractive aspect of our national character – all the more so as so many of their fellow citizens seem by now to have given it up. It seems to me that, with the empire gone, our 21st-century prime ministers have somehow persuaded themselves that, because Britain has a veto in the Security Council, it is still some kind of a great power (even if not a Great Power). In reality, as everyone knows, our seat at the UN's top table is a reflection of the international situation nearly seventy years ago and it seems certain to disappear – unlamented so far as I am concerned – in the course of the next twenty or so years.

Our present situation reminds me very much of where we were in the 1960s. At that time we had sizeable responsibilities and commitments overseas, but the end of the empire was in sight and it was clear to all with eyes to see that we did not have the resources to maintain a naval or military presence east of Suez. Plans to carry out the necessary withdrawal were fiercely resisted in some quarters: but those in charge (notably the Chancellor Roy Jenkins and the Defence Secretary Denis Healey) were clear-sighted about what needed to be done and by the time the Wilson government left office the process of withdrawal, which had been started by Macmillan, was well under way. I am not aware of anyone around today who thinks that this was a mistake.

Anthony Eden's Egyptian adventure in 1956 and the devaluation of 1967 were the triggers for the change in our 'East of Suez' policy. In the same way, I believe that the Iraq war and what I am afraid I can only call the fiasco of the allied intervention in Afghanistan, the 2009 banking crisis and the House of Commons' refusal in September 2013 to endorse military intervention in Syria, together provide both the need and the opportunity for a strategic alteration in our foreign policy today. My hope is that the generation that has grown to maturity since the millennium will pay heed to the appalling record of the twentieth century; that it will decide that we should work with others through whatever channels are available to resolve conflict, wherever it occurs, by non-military means; and that this will become the bedrock of British foreign policy.

I am aware of course that, human nature being what it is, this approach will not of itself bring armed conflict or external aggression to an end – as events in the Middle East and Ukraine in 2014 have all too clearly demonstrated. That is why I believe in maintaining a strong defensive capability, including our own nuclear deterrent. But I am convinced that, as the geopolitical balance of resources and power shifts in the coming generation, we should rule out any use of British armed forces for intervention in the affairs of another country, except where this is strictly necessary for the fulfilment of our obligations under the UN or NATO (or any successor body). I believe that neither our history nor our supposed 'military prowess' provide any grounds for our aspiring to the role of world policeman, either alone or as the junior partner of the USA; and that, like it or not, we should accept this as a fact of life and devote more attention to honing our diplomatic skills, which seem in danger of falling into disuse. The harm done by misconceived intervention in Iraq and Afghanistan – and, it seems, in Libya too – has in my view been profound and lasting, and the lesson should be learned. It is ironic to recall that the Foreign Office used to be criticised for having too many Arabists on its staff; it seems to me, in the light of the mistakes made in recent years, that it must have had too few.

If I read them aright, the German people, in coming to grips with their own troubled past, are already deeply committed to the kind of approach I favour and it would be fitting if we were to embark on a joint endeavour on these lines to coincide with the centenary of the outbreak of the First World War. I feel very strongly that modern Germany and Britain are now natural allies and I believe our foreign policy should reflect this. In summer 2014 I attended a choral concert in the awe-inspiring splendour of Westminster Hall where the singers were drawn from the Parliament Choir (to which a number of my friends belong) and their opposite numbers from the German Bundestag choir. The concert was held to mark the centenary and during Mendelssohn's '*Lobgesang*' the two choirs sang unaccompanied some verses from the hymn '*Nun Danket Alle Gott*' ('Now Thank We All Our God'), which it is thought the soldiers of both countries may have sung together when they emerged briefly from their trenches during Christmas 1914. In his speech before the concert the President of the Bundestag, Professor Norbert Lammert, referring to the 1914–18 war and what followed fifteen years later, said, 'I can assure you that we Germans have learned our lesson from those events.' It was the first time I had ever heard a German politician use that particular phrase and I am as near certain as it is possible to be that he is right.

Like many of my generation I am a committed Europhile. Just as the First World War was said to be a war to end all wars, so the Second was, for us, a war to end all European wars. Once in the 1970s my wife Doreen and I stopped at Verdun on our way to a meeting in the Strasburg Parliament. In 1916 three quarters of a million French and German soldiers were killed at Verdun and many of their bones lie unidentified in a common ossuary on the battlefield. To see the flags of France, Germany and the European Union flying together by the ossuary was, for me, an unforgettable sight. To a later generation this may seem simply sentimental, but it lies at the heart of my support for the European Union and of my conception of Britain's place in the 21st-century world and is based, I believe, on a proper understanding of history – a subject which receives too little attention these days and is easily forgotten in the contemporary arguments about the shortcomings of the Brussels bureaucracy and similar subjects of second order importance.

Looking ahead, I cannot see a secure future for Britain if it is wholly dependent on the changing moods and demography of a United States which is increasingly uncertain how best to adapt to its own new geopolitical situation. I remain convinced that the right course for this country is to remain in the European Union. In troubled times it may be very lonely indeed outside.

–CHAPTER THREE–

BALLIOL

I WENT UP TO Balliol in 1938 and took to it like a duck to water. The college had a huge – and lasting – influence on me and, as I look back, I find it hard to credit that I spent only two years there – one before the war and the other, six years later, after it had ended.

Balliol men are sometimes said to have a high opinion of themselves. There may be a smidgeon of truth in this – it was, after all, Balliol men whom Herbert Asquith famously described as possessing 'the tranquil consciousness of an effortless superiority'. But if there were any such feelings of superiority in my day they had nothing to do with anyone's social background. There were of course no women undergraduates at the college and the English class system was at its apogee: but, within these limitations, Balliol had a wider social and ethnic mix than most other colleges. There was an open and inclusive atmosphere, where people were accepted on their own merits and not because of school or other connections – something which was not so common in pre-war days as it may have since become. There were a number of Etonians (though none, I think, who joined the Bullingdon) and most of the major public schools were represented: but there were many grammar school boys, as well as a sizeable contingent from Glasgow, reared in the very different Scottish education system. There was also a strong connection with the United States and with India – Balliol probably had more undergraduates from the sub-continent than all the other colleges put together. The college war memorial also includes the name of one of the first German Rhodes Scholars to come to Oxford after the First World War: Adam von Trott, whom the Nazis hanged in 1944 when the bomb plot against Hitler misfired.

Relations between Fellows and undergraduates were good – somewhat detached, as was the custom in those more hierarchical days, but easy-going and founded on mutual respect. The Senior Common Room was a strong one. The doyen was Cyril Bailey, an admired figure who was perhaps the most distinguished classicist of his day; and in Humphrey Sumner, Dick Southern and Christopher Hill the college had three historians of unusual quality, all of whom became college heads after the war. We freshmen appreciated the intellectual distinction that these and other Fellows brought to the college community we had joined: but, for most of us, interest in the SCR more or less ended there.

Tutorials and lectures were a novel and quite agreeable way of filling a morning but in what seemed increasingly likely to be the last year of European peace, academic work was not the first priority. What we really wanted to do was to get to know our peers and sit up half the night discussing the great issues of the extraordinary times in which our generation lived. Though not noted for its architectural beauty, Balliol was well designed for this purpose. With around 300 undergraduates (of whom over eighty were in their first year) it was big enough to be more or less self-sufficient socially. Freshmen all lived in college, where the centrally situated buttery, with a good stretch of lawn for outside drinking, provided a natural meeting point. It was an intrinsically friendly place.

The general style of the college was greatly influenced by Sandy Lindsay,[6] a humane and liberal-minded Scot who by 1938 had been Master for nearly fifteen years. Lindsay had strong views about the responsibilities young men at places like Balliol had towards their less privileged fellow citizens and society at large. His views were in tune with those of men who had grown up in the decade of the Jarrow hunger march and, when I went up, Balliol was a highly political place – more so, I believe, than any other college at the time.

The prevailing ethos was left of centre, but there were relatively few Marxists in the college and Conservative supporters of the 'Middle Way' advocated by Harold

6 In 1945 he was made a Labour peer, Lord Lindsay of Birker. His wife did not approve and from then on formal invitations to the Master's Lodgings came from 'Lord Lindsay and Mrs Lindsay'

Macmillan[7] (whose son, Maurice, was one of the 1938 entry) were generally comfortable with Lindsay's ideas. As the Michaelmas term began, the ink was scarcely dry on the Munich Agreement and political discussion focused almost entirely on issues of foreign rather than domestic policy. When Lindsay stood in the Oxford by-election of November 1938, as an independent candidate on an anti-Munich platform, he received overwhelming support from undergraduates of all political persuasions. During the ensuing year party political differences among undergraduates were not very important; what mattered was the position you took on Chamberlain's appeasement policy. Four students of my time who became prominent politicians in later life were the future Prime Minister, Edward Heath; the then Communist Party member Denis Healey, who became a Labour Cabinet minister; Julian Amery, who led the right wing Suez Group in the 1950s; and Roy Jenkins, who founded the Social Democratic Party. As a cross-party quartet this would be hard to beat.

My outside activities, which I pursued enthusiastically, included debating in the Union, where I was elected to membership of the Library Committee (the bottom end of the Union's greasy pole) in my first year; but for the war I would probably have given a good deal of time to the Union, where Balliol then had almost a monopoly of

7 In an article in the 1920s he floated the idea of moving to a system 'which lay between unadulterated free enterprise and collectivism' and called this the Middle Way

the senior posts. I also sang in the university's Bach Choir under the baton of Sir Thomas Armstrong – whose son, Robert, with whom I worked quite closely in the 1960s, became in turn principal private secretary to Roy Jenkins at the Treasury and Ted Heath at No. 10 and Cabinet Secretary under Margaret Thatcher (when he made famous the concept of being 'economical with the truth'[8]). Having inherited a decent voice from my mother Chrissie, who in a later generation would have been a professional singer, I had sung in my school choir in the Matthew Passion alongside Ian Wallace – later an operatic bass, now long dead but perhaps still remembered by a few for his rendition of Flanders and Swann's Hippopotamus song: 'Mud, mud, glorious mud, nothing quite like it for cooling the blood'. I also took part in the Balliol Players' production of Aristophanes's *The Birds*, which toured schools and other venues in southern England during the long vacation. Ted Heath was the producer, Madron Seligman (a future MEP) the stage manager and the music was written by my fellow freshman Geoffrey Bush, who later became a composer of some note. I was a member of the chorus – as was Roy Jenkins, who gave an impressive imitation of a bird about to leave the ground, which those who knew him only in later life might find hard to credit.

Roy and I met on our first day at Balliol and remained close friends until he died sixty-five years later; and happily

8 In the Australian *Spycatcher* case in 1986

the friendship has continued with Jennifer and their family since his death. Leaving aside his distinguished record as politician, statesman and author, Roy's gift for personal friendship was one of his most notable characteristics. The breadth of his intellectual interests and his ever-present sense of the absurd made him extraordinarily good company among close friends. In private conversation there was no trace of self-importance; indeed, as time went on, he often indulged in an engaging form of self-deprecation – it being understood by those who knew him well that such self-deprecation was not to be taken too literally. His father, a former coal-miner in the Welsh valleys, was by then an MP and Clement Attlee's PPS, and Roy's interest in politics was well established. Our friendship was personal and not political but I can remember scarcely any important political issue on which we held significantly different views and I have a huge admiration for his contribution to public life. As a freshman at Balliol Roy was well liked and in his final year he was elected president of the Junior Common Room.

Apart from Roy my closest friend was Neil Bruce, a handsome, debonair young man who caused many female hearts to flutter. His father had held university posts in Australia and in Lahore, when it was still part of undivided India, and perhaps because of this Neil became a dedicated globetrotter. His first job after the war was as a university lecturer in Memphis, Tennessee; he then became a foreign correspondent for the BBC in Europe, the Middle East and Africa, and wrote an eye-witness account of the Portuguese revolution of 1974.[9] Unlike Roy, Neil and I both went back to Oxford after the war. For some months in 1946 we shared agreeable lodgings opposite the University Church in the High Street, where we each had a bedroom on the top floor with joint use of an elegant sitting room on the floor below. This is now a luxurious bedroom in the excellent Old Bank Hotel and no doubt the question of a commemorative plaque is under consideration.

Another lifelong friendship which started towards the end of my first year was with Madron Seligman, the stage-manager of *The Birds*. Madron was a man of extraordinary charm, who was the life and soul of any party he attended. He was a talented musician and if there was a piano within reach he would, when the right moment arrived, go to the keyboard and play whatever music seemed most suited to the prevailing mood. With typical panache he took his own piano with him when he went to war. By some astonishing piece of sleight of hand it accompanied him in the Sixth Armoured Division to North Africa and was shipped from there to Italy, where, after surviving the fighting at Monte Cassino, it was left behind. Many years after the war Madron's mother tracked it down and I understand that it is now in regular use in his daughter's house in Carinthia. Madron was also Ted Heath's closest friend and, with his

9 *Portugal: The Last Empire* (David and Charles, 1975)

American wife Nancy-Joan and their family, a benign influence on Heath's personal life.

The Balliol I went back to after the war seemed very different from the one I had previously known, though this may have had more to do with changes in me than in the college. I was by then twenty-six – distinctly elderly for an undergraduate – and Oxford was full of galloping majors and squadron-leaders of roughly the same age, more like dons than undergraduates. It must have seemed a strange and rather daunting place to any eighteen-year-old going up to the university straight from school.

One way in which it differed from the college I had previously known was that relations between Fellows and undergraduates became much closer. Having switched to PPE[10] when I returned in January 1946, I was tutored in economics (my main subject) by Tommy Balogh, with whom I remained on friendly terms long after I left Oxford. Balogh, a Hungarian by both birth and temperament, created controversy wherever he went and the often sensible advice he gave to Harold Wilson and other ministers in the 1960s and 70s was less persuasive than it could have been because of the extreme way in which he expressed his views. As a tutor I found him outstanding – one of the two best teachers I have

10 Philosophy, Politics and Economics

ever encountered. His original mind and unorthodox ways of expressing his trenchant views gave me an understanding of the supposedly dry subject of economics from which I benefited throughout my working life. His impish sense of humour and complete lack of respect for conventional ways of thinking made him excellent company (as Hungarians so often are) both as a tutor and a friend. I have therefore thought it worthwhile reproducing in Appendix I a review I wrote for the *Balliol Record* of June Morris's excellent biography of Balogh, *A Macaw Among Mandarins*.

Balogh also unwittingly gave me useful tutorials in the ways of the land of his birth. In 1977 I paid the first of several visits to that remarkable country as a member of the British–Hungarian Round Table, of which Mark Bonham-Carter[11] (whom I succeeded in 1980) was then co-chairman. The government-sponsored Round Table's purpose was to keep some active links between the two countries alive during the later stages of the Cold War. It met once a year, in Britain and Hungary alternately. On this occasion we met in Pecs, a delightful university town south of Budapest, which seemed to me exactly as it must have been in the reign of the Austro-Hungarian Emperor (or rather, in the case of Hungary, the King) Franz Josef. I found the Hungarian people – with their ability to charm and infuriate the visitor in almost equal measure – excellent company and over the years developed quite an affection for them.

11 1922–94. Chairman, Race Relations Board, 1966–70. Later Lord Bonham-Carter

The twelve-man British delegation consisted mainly of MPs, academics and journalists; their Hungarian counterparts were drawn from similar sections of society and, though there were some apparatchiks among them, there were no obvious secret policemen. The Hungarian co-chairman was Ivan Behrend, a distinguished economist of great charisma who had recently been invited to spend six months at All Souls College, Oxford. He stood out from the rest for the quality of his intellect and made no secret of his strong desire to see Hungary develop closer relations with the West. These were the end-years of Janos Kadar's presidency. He was the man the Russians sent to Budapest to run the country after they had quashed the revolution of 1956 and it was widely thought – I am sure correctly – that he later did a deal with his Soviet masters which gave him a very free hand in the country's internal affairs on condition that he followed Moscow's line on foreign policy with unqualified loyalty. In the 1980s I chaired a meeting at the CBI which he addressed during an official visit to London. He came across to me on that occasion as an old-fashioned, hard-line Communist who was able to adopt two quite different personalities according to whether the matters under discussion were internal or external affairs and thus, with typical Hungarian mental agility, to keep both his compatriots and the Russians happy.

I made three new friends in this period to whom I became particularly close. One was Gordon Samuels who, soon after receiving his Oxford law degree, moved to Sydney, where he became a Supreme Court Judge, was Chancellor of its principal university for eighteen years and in 1996 was appointed State Governor – thus becoming, so far as I know, the only Balliol man who took literally his fellow alumnus Hilaire Belloc's advice to 'go out and govern New South Wales'.[12] Gordon was hugely respected in Australia for the quality of his mind and his integrity and despite living most of our lives in different hemispheres we remained in close touch until Gordon died in 2007.

Another man who became one of my best, lifelong friends was Roy Macnab, a South African who served in the Royal Navy during the war in HMS *Petard*, which famously forced a U-boat to the surface and relieved it of its Enigma code books before it sank, with two British sailors on board. After the war Roy went to Jesus College, Oxford where he met his future wife Rachel and he never returned to South Africa to live. He did, however, maintain strong links with the country of his birth and became a leading figure in its literary life, both as an admired poet and as the author of a number of interesting books about South Africa's interface with Europe. Roy, who died in 2004, was an exceptionally

12 *Cautionary Tales*. 'Sir, you have disappointed us/We had intended you to be/the next Prime Minister but three/The stocks were sold, the press was squared/the middle class was quite prepared/But as it is...my language fails/Go out and govern New South Wales'

nice human being and our enduring friendship with him and his family was very important to Doreen and me.

My third new friend was Bill Ash, a maverick Texan whose schooldays left him with a lifelong desire to punish bullies. This led him to cross the border into Canada in December 1939 in order to join the air force and fight on the British side in the war, in which his own country was not of course involved at that time. Arriving in Britain in early 1941, he flew Spitfires for fifteen months until he was shot down over France and eventually taken prisoner. He spent the rest of the war as a serial escaper, making thirteen attempted home runs (some very nearly successful) and narrowly avoiding death at the hands of the Gestapo. In 1946 he became a student at Balliol, from where he applied to join the Communist Party of Great Britain but was turned down because he was considered to be a Marxist-Leninist deviationist. Bill was great company.[13]

During the third term of my post-war incarnation I was elected president of the Junior Common Room, an honour which I much appreciated. However, I never actually took on the job. Shortly after the JCR election I sat and passed the exam for entry into the civil service and was offered a

13 His autobiography *A Red Square* (Howard Baker; London, 1978) is a good read

post starting in January 1947. In retrospect it seems to me that this sequence of events gave me the best of both worlds – the pleasure of knowing that my fellow undergraduates wanted me to lead their self-governing body, without the chore of actually doing the job. At the end of this same term, in December 1946, I took the first half of the exam papers for my Oxford degree, with the second half to be taken in the following March. In the first half, while I was still at Oxford, I performed satisfactorily but in the second half, which I took after being away from my books and at work in Whitehall for a clear three months, I achieved a distinction. There must be a moral of some kind in this.

So ended my second incarnation at Balliol. In April 1947, nine years after I first took up residence there, Oxford gave me an Honours degree in which (under the peculiar rules applicable to those whose studies had been interrupted by the war) no classes were awarded. Once again, perhaps this gave me the best of all worlds since no one can prove that, if classes had been awarded, I would not have got a First.

As I have already made clear, I admire my old college and owe a great deal to it. This has nothing to do with any real or imagined 'effortless superiority'. It reflects my view of what the college stands for, its values and attitudes of mind – among them inclusiveness, social responsibility and openness to new ideas – and the consistency with which it has been able to pass these on from generation to generation. In 2013 Balliol celebrated its 750th anniversary. The college put on a rich and varied series of events at home and overseas, which were masterminded by the recently appointed Master, Sir Drummond Bone. Having seen him in action at several of these and got to know him personally, I am sure this ancient institution and its values are in good hands

–CHAPTER FOUR–

MERCHANT NAVY

IN OCTOBER 1939 Roy Jenkins's father, who was always ready to use his influence as an MP to help his son's friends, found me a berth in the Merchant Navy. When war broke out the government took control of all ship movements and decisions on the cargo they carried were taken by the Ministry of War Transport, but the management of individual ships was left to their owners or to shipping companies appointed by the government to run them. Through his local contacts in South Wales Arthur arranged for the South American Saint Line, a go-ahead Cardiff shipping company whose joint managing directors were Lord Howard de Walden and an entrepreneurial man of business Dick Street, to take me on as a cadet.

The Saint Line, as it was commonly known, had been formed as recently as 1936, following the merger of two shipping companies with which Street had been involved. The plan was to run a regular service between South Wales and Argentina, carrying coal for the British-owned railways to Buenos Aires and returning to Britain with bulk grain from Rosario. With Lord Howard de Walden's financial backing, Street had put together a fleet of modern cargo liners of innovative design with which he hoped to establish a southbound sailing every ten days. These plans were, of course, overtaken by the war in which twelve of the Saint Line's sixteen ships were sunk by enemy action.

My first ship was the *Saint Rosario*, which had been built in 1937 and was specially designed to serve the shallow draught harbour of Rosario, a major grain port some six hours steaming upriver from Buenos Aires. The ship had a crew of thirty, made up of eight officers, three petty officers, ten seamen, five engine-room hands, three catering staff – and me. I ate with the officers: but to begin with, as a first voyager, I spent most of my working time under the supervision of our kindly Greek boatswain, learning to perform such mundane tasks as scrubbing decks, handling mooring ropes, climbing the rigging and, above all in wartime, keeping look-out.

The seamen thought it odd to have a toff like me on board as a cadet, but they seem to have soon concluded (incorrectly, I hasten to say) that I had put a young relative of Lord Howard de Walden 'in the family way' and been sent to sea to keep me out of further mischief. Thereafter, they accepted me as a fellow worker without more ado and were unfailingly helpful in showing me the ropes. In this, as in other ways, they exhibited a tolerant spirit which I came to admire in my fellow mariners of all ranks. Merchant ships have small crews who often spend months at a time away from home and, over the generations, seamen appear to have developed a culture which recognises the need for them to get on with one another reasonably well. It is certainly true that in my six years in the Merchant Navy I never witnessed serious quarrels among my shipmates of the kind that often poison relationships ashore. They may not always have liked or admired everyone on board but a 'live and let live' philosophy seemed to be deeply rooted in their attitude to their shipmates.

The most difficult of the seaman's skills I had to learn was probably helmsmanship. The *Saint Rosario* did not have any quartermasters, one of whom in larger ships would always be at the steering wheel. Our wheel was taken for an hour at a time (because the work could require intense concentration) by able seamen on watch – or by the new cadet. I took my first turn at this duty, under the vigilant eye of the officer of the watch, while we were in a westbound North Atlantic convoy in severe November weather. All ships naturally sailed without lights of any kind and I found that, in the dark, simply keeping the stern of the ship ahead in sight, when it was at one moment on the crest of an enormous wave and at the next invisible on its far side, was by no means easy. Fortunately I was born with good sea legs and was never troubled by sea sickness, and we all relished heavy seas, which made it difficult for German U-boats to launch a torpedo at us successfully. There was also gun crew duty. In the first few months of the war all merchant ships were fitted with a 4-inch gun, usually of 1914–18 vintage, for use against any U-boat which surfaced close to them. Since this was a very rare occurrence the guns were little used, but the seamen and I were trained to fire our elderly armament by an equally elderly Royal Marine steward (or 'flunkey' as they were called) who had been brought out of retirement for this purpose.

Air attacks against merchant ships were frequent in British coastal waters and the primitive anti-aircraft weapons with which we were equipped in the early days of the war were usually manned by army personnel, who came on board when we sailed from East Coast ports, such as London or Hull, on our way to the Atlantic via the north of Scotland. Before we left British waters somewhere in the western approaches these maritime soldiers were disembarked so that they could make the return journey defending some other, homeward-bound ship. We didn't envy them their job.

When I had, fairly quickly, gained enough experience of the seamen's routine, I was initiated by the officers into the more sophisticated aspects of their craft, notably navigation. This, at which in time I became decently proficient, is both a science and an art; experience and intuition both play a part in it, especially in bad weather or poor visibility. For me, by far the most interesting aspect was celestial navigation – the somewhat arcane process of plotting one's position by 'taking sights' of the sun or stars with a sextant and calculating from these, by quite elaborate algebraic formulae, where exactly in a vast, featureless ocean the ship is located at any given time.

It quite often happens that an ocean-going ship passes several days without sighting either sun or stars, in which case the navigator plots its estimated position by 'dead reckoning', which at best provides only approximate results and at worst can be quite wide of the mark. Occasionally at times like this, a patch of cloud may clear briefly to reveal a single star, which gives the navigator a chance to use his specialist skills. With a bit of luck and the help of his logarithm tables he may be able to identify the star and, though this will not enable him to plot his position at once, it will set him on his way to doing so. This process is by no means easy and, if successfully accomplished, brings with it both a useful outcome and a satisfying sense of achievement. [I write in the present tense as if the conditions I experienced still existed. In fact, of course, navigation has been transformed by the introduction of modern technology. Much of what I have described is now carried out, more reliably, by a computer rather than a ship's officer trying to keep his balance on a heaving bridge. It must have taken a lot of the satisfaction my contemporaries and I experienced out of the navigation process.]

My first voyage on the *Saint Rosario* began on a bleak day in November 1939 as we set sail from Barry Docks – a Victorian port in South Wales which has turned bleakness into an art form. With a cargo of Welsh anthracite on board we were bound for Argentina, where we were due to load canned meat and other provisions for the return journey to Britain. Despite our South American destination, we started our voyage by heading northwest in order to join a North Atlantic convoy. The seas we encountered in that first part of our voyage were, as I have said, mountainous, and we were more concerned with maintaining our proper station in the convoy and keeping track of the signals sent by the convoy Commodore (a retired Admiral on board the leading merchant ship) than with spotting U-boats.

Convoys were, of course, a complete novelty, not just to first voyagers like me but to the captains and crews of all the naval escorts and merchant ships involved. At that stage of the war convoys were much smaller than they later became – which was just as well, as they were for a while distinctly amateur affairs, with some ships which always seemed to be out of line and others which kept dropping astern with engine trouble of one kind or another. The little corvettes, which made up the bulk of our naval escorts and were tossed about like rubber ducks by the stormy seas, were kept continuously busy rounding up the stragglers.

When we were about 500 miles clear of the United Kingdom we took our leave of the convoy and proceeded independently towards the north-eastern tip of South America. As we headed south, the seas moderated and before long we were steaming through calm tropical waters under the benign gaze of the constellation of the Southern Cross, which I was seeing for the first time. These waters were at that time beyond the reach of U-boats and the only risk of enemy action was from a heavy cruiser or other surface raider of the German fleet.

As it happened – though at the time we didn't know it – a powerful German raider was at large in precisely the area we were heading for. The pocket battleship *Admiral Graf Spee* had sailed from Germany to the South Atlantic a few days before the war began, with orders to offer 'a constant but elusive' threat to Allied merchant ships and so draw away heavy ships of the Royal Navy which could ill be spared from the Home Fleet. In this, the *Graf Spee*'s highly experienced commander, Captain Hans Langsdorff, did an excellent job.[14]

He sank his first British ship off Pernambuco in Brazil at the end of September 1939, after which he steered eastwards for the unprotected route off the west coast of Africa where he sank four ships in October, then doubled back into the South Atlantic and destroyed another ship, before ceasing operations and lying low for a while to confuse the Royal Navy. He then made a short incursion into the Indian Ocean, where he sank another couple of ships, before returning to the South Atlantic and sinking two more at the beginning of December. One of these managed to signal its position before being forced to cease wireless communication

14 See David Miller, *Langsdorff and the River Plate* (Pen and Sword, 2013)

and this finally led to Admiral Harwood's force of three cruisers (*Achilles*, *Ajax* and *Exeter*) catching up with him off the River Plate.

Although the *Graf Spee* outgunned all three British ships, they succeeded – in spite of heavy damage to HMS *Exeter*, which was eventually forced to withdraw from the battle – in inflicting sufficient damage on the German ship to force Langsdorff to seek temporary refuge in the neutral port of Montevideo. In the next few days the British Minister to Uruguay, Sir Eugen Millington-Drake, conducted a skilful campaign of disinformation about the presence of non-existent British warships off the River Plate, which persuaded its captain to scuttle the *Graf Spee*. It seems clear that Langsdorff took this decision to avoid leading his crew to what he thought would be certain destruction. He was evidently an honourable and compassionate man, who did his best to make sure that the crews of Allied merchant ships he sank had a good chance of making it to the coast in their lifeboats; and no doubt in order to avoid accusations that he scuttled his ship to save his own life, he committed suicide – his body wrapped in a German naval ensign – in his hotel room in Montevideo.

As a result, when we reached the scene a few days after the battle, we were greeted by the welcome sight of the *Graf Spee* resting on the bottom of the River Plate with only a gun turret showing above the water. This was the first example of the remarkable run of good luck which I enjoyed throughout the war.

The Buenos Aires in which we spent the next three weeks, while discharging and loading our cargo, was an elegant and sophisticated city for which its description as the Paris of the southern hemisphere was not altogether far-fetched. There was a large and influential British community, whose members held the top jobs in the railways, the public utilities and other commercial activities and relaxed in exclusive clubs, where English was the only language spoken and officers from Allied ships were warmly welcomed. Relations between the two governments were good but I suspect that the British, with their often superior airs, were respected rather than loved; and as Britain liquidated its overseas investments (including the Argentine railways) to pay for the war, its influence in a country where a high proportion of the population was of Italian or German stock sharply declined. This was very noticeable when I revisited the country in 1943, shortly after the military coup that brought the future President Juan Perón to prominence and sowed the seeds of the anti-British sentiment that ultimately led to the Falklands war of 1982.

When loading was complete we set off independently across the South Atlantic for Freetown in Sierra Leone, where the homeward-bound convoys assembled. Freetown was an insalubrious outpost of empire and crews normally remained on their ships while waiting for their convoy to depart, but somehow I managed to contract malaria and had to go to hospital in the town. My temperature rose to dizzy heights and I can still remember wondering – with interest rather than anxiety – in my delirium whether my twenty-year life was about to come to an end. Happily, it didn't and as our convoy had taken longer than expected to assemble I was able to get back on board my ship before she departed. The malaria has never returned.

After making our way home a fair distance off the west coast of occupied Europe and rounding Britain 'north-about', our voyage ended in Gravesend. When darkness fell, we watched from the safety of our ship while the Luftwaffe bombed the City of London and the entire sky lit up with the flames of burning buildings – a spectacular sight from 10 miles away and a reminder to us travellers of the dangers the people of London had to face in those early days of the Blitz.

I did two more voyages in the *Saint Rosario* – one to Argentina and one to Brazil – and one, to Canada, in her sister ship the *Saint Clears*. Luckily for me, I didn't continue in the *Saint Clears* which, after I left her, was sent to Murmansk with supplies for our new allies, the Russians. Having discharged her cargo she set off for home but, owing to some miscalculation by the port authorities, she was trapped in the ice about 20 miles into her journey and it was three months before an ice-breaker was able to free her. A former shipmate, whom I had introduced to the great classics of Russian literature, which I was devouring at the time, told me that he had read *War and Peace* right through twice during this period of enforced idleness.

In these early years of the war the Battle of the Atlantic swung violently to and fro, with the balance of advantage favouring one side or the other in turn. Churchill said that the only thing that really frightened him during the war was the U-boat peril; sailing in the North Atlantic convoys, it was not difficult to understand why. The fall of France in June 1940 gave Germany a huge advantage by making new bases available for the maintenance and repair of U-boats and shortening the distance to the mid-Atlantic target areas; and this was quickly reflected in increased losses of Allied shipping. The convoys of which we were part came regularly under attack and on my third Atlantic crossing I witnessed the sinking of a tanker filled with aviation fuel which, when torpedoed, exploded in a ball of fire and was gone in a couple of minutes – not something I want to see again. However, before the end of the year the balance was redressed by the exchange of fifty old US destroyers for British naval bases in the western hemisphere, and this substantially enhanced the Royal Navy's ability to protect the North Atlantic convoys. From then on these became much larger, with a corresponding increase in the number of escorts assigned to each.

This in turn led the German naval command to develop the tactic of U-boats hunting in 'wolf packs', which for a while caused devastating losses of Allied ships. New measures, such as the occupation of Iceland and the use of long-range aircraft to close the mid-Atlantic 'air gap', helped to counter the wolf packs. But I think it is fair to say that all the two navies could really achieve on their own was to hold each other to a draw: it was the cryptographers of Bletchley Park who eventually won the battle.

On my return home in a convoy from Halifax, Nova Scotia to Liverpool in September 1941, I was transferred to the *Saint Essylt*, a brand new diesel-powered ship built in Sunderland, which during her short life was the pride of the Saint Line fleet. By the time I joined her, on my twenty-second birthday, I was quite an experienced sailor, comfortable with my job and my shipmates, and I was pleased to be part of the ship's company of such an up-to-date vessel on her maiden voyage. What I didn't know was that I was about to embark on an unplanned voyage round the world.

The assignment we were given for the maiden voyage was to take military equipment and stores to Allied troops in Singapore. With France out of the war, the Mediterranean was closed to through traffic so we had to go the long way round, via the Cape of Good Hope. After the lengthy voyage south we refuelled at Durban, where the famous soprano, Perle Gibson, sang through the public address system to more than five thousand South African troops as they left for the Middle East. We then spent a few days in Bombay loading extra stores – and as it turned out bringing smallpox on board – before leaving for Singapore.

We were at sea when we heard the news that the capital ships HMS *Prince of Wales* and *Repulse* had both been sunk by aircraft of the Japanese invading force. I can still vividly remember the shock and incredulity with which we greeted the news – it was as if Buckingham Palace and the Bank of England had both been razed to the ground in a single London air raid. So we were not surprised when we received orders to make for Fremantle in Western Australia instead of Singapore. Thirty-six hours later Singapore fell and we realised just how close we had come to walking down the gangway into a Japanese prison camp. Once again my luck had held.

By then we knew that our well-liked second officer, Alan Brightwell, had caught smallpox in Bombay. He was a quiet, rather studious man belonging to a strict non-conformist sect in Wales, and we gathered that he and his family objected to vaccination on religious grounds. He died shortly after we changed course to bypass Singapore and we buried him at sea – always a moving ceremony.

It had fallen to me to take the patient his food and to carry out the minimal nursing services we were able to offer him and so, although my vaccination was right up to date and I had no symptoms of the disease, it was decided when we arrived at Fremantle that it would be prudent to leave me behind while the *Saint Essylt* continued on her way to whatever destination she was directed to next. I was accordingly taken to the quarantine station on a small island off Fremantle, where I spent four not unpleasant but rather boring weeks, which gave the doctors time to establish that I had not in fact contracted the disease.

At the end of this period during which, as the only resident in the quarantine station, I was royally looked after by the nursing staff, I flew to South Australia to join my next ship. This was the *Lycaon*, an old stalwart of the Blue Funnel Line, built in 1913 for the China trade. Founded in 1866 by the Liverpool company Alfred Holt, the Blue Funnel Line (whose ships were all named after real or mythical figures of ancient Greece) was one of the oldest and most distinguished shipping lines in Britain. In 1939 it had a fleet of seventy-six ships, of which forty-one were sunk by enemy action in the war.

The *Lycaon* was docked in Port Pirie, a smallish port on the Spencer Gulf north of Adelaide, loading iron ore – guaranteed to take the ship to the bottom quickly if torpedoed

– for the journey home. The officers and deck crew were British and the engine-room and catering staff Chinese. As there was no place for a cadet on the *Lycaon* the authorities decided that I would work my passage home as an ordinary seaman, which suited me fine as it would enlarge my experience. At the start there were a few, not too serious, attempts to take the mickey out of the posh boy – including sending me up to paint the more or less inaccessible and mildly terrifying upper reaches of the topmast when we got to Sydney Harbour – but they were soon dropped and I was accepted as a slightly eccentric but otherwise normal member of the team.

In my spare time I found a congenial companion in the Radio Officer, who was a Wykehamist and had perhaps become a wartime sailor for similar reasons to my own. Off watch on the voyage home we enjoyed many conversations about Tolstoy, Jane Austen and E. M. Forster and other subjects which we had in common.

From Sydney we sailed to Port Lyttleton and Dunedin to pick up more cargo for Britain and I got my first sight of New Zealand's beautiful south island. Then we made our way towards the Atlantic and home by way of Cape Horn. Rounding the Horn is something virtually all sailors would be pleased to do and I was no exception. As it happened, the day in question was fine and the sea dead calm (just as it was when I rounded North Cape in a Norwegian cruise ship fifty years later). The famous sight lost nothing by this. Cape Horn itself is, of course, a small island at the end of a little archipelago which stretches southward from the solid mass of Tierra del Fuego. In the clear sunlight of the day we rounded it, the sight of the huge continental range of the Andes descending gradually from far away in the north to the tiny Horn Island beside us was something to be indelibly imprinted in one's memory.

Once round the corner we headed northeast for the long crossing of the South Atlantic as we made for Freetown to join a convoy to the UK. What happened after we left Freetown has been described by Stephen Roskill, the official historian of the war at sea, in his book on the Blue Funnel Line, *A Merchant Fleet in War*.[15]

> The convoy[16] consisted initially of thirty-seven ships and had four escort vessels and an Armed Merchant Cruiser with it. Like all Sierra Leone convoys it was a slow one and had difficulty in maintaining seven knots. On 17 August, the eleventh day out, U-boat attacks began and we now know that the convoy was unlucky enough to fall foul of a group of seven boats which were on their way south to the Freetown area. During the next two days four ships and the

15 Collins, 1962

16 This was convoy SL 118. In 2013 it was featured, as a typical Atlantic convoy, in an excellent exhibition about the Battle of the Atlantic on board HQS *Wellington*, which had been an escort ship for SL 118 and is now the headquarters of the Honourable Company of Master Mariners, moored off Victoria Embankment in London

> armed Merchant Cruiser were torpedoed and three of the former were sunk. On 23 August the escort was reinforced and the convoy divided into fast and slow groups. The *Lycaon*, which had picked up sixty survivors from the sunk ships [*including many from a Dutch ship immediately ahead of us in the convoy line, some of whom died on board the* Lycaon] arrived safely in Greenock on 25 August.

And so my unplanned round-the-world voyage ended exactly eleven months after it began.

After my world trip I had enough sea-time under my belt to sit for my second mate's certificate, the lowest qualification on the road to becoming a Master Mariner. So when I left the *Lycaon* I stayed ashore and, after some home leave with my family, I got accommodation at Liverpool University, with which the Nautical College where I was to prepare for and take the exam had close links. All went well and I emerged with one stripe on the sleeve of my uniform to become Third (that is, most junior) Officer on my old ship, the *Saint Rosario*.

Before long we were off the coast of Brazil where we called at several ports, from Pernambuco in the north to Porto Allegro in the south. I found it an interesting and stimulating country, somehow more optimistic than Argentina, and took the opportunity of a free weekend to visit Sao

Paulo, making the forty-mile journey on a British-built mountain railway from the southern port of Santos. Even then, with only ten million inhabitants, Sao Paulo was a megalopolis and, though I have never been back, I am glad I went because it seems to me that one cannot understand Brazil – always the country of the future, never the present – without having seen it.

I was comfortable being back on my old ship but by the end of the voyage I became restless and decided I needed a change. So at the end of the voyage I arranged a transfer to a ship owned by John Holt & Co. of Liverpool (no relation to Alfred Holt of the Blue Funnel Line) which traded mainly with West Africa. The one voyage I made on this ship was the occasion of the narrowest shave I had during my whole war. We were anchored in the river Humber one evening, awaiting entry to Hull, when a lone German aircraft, returning from a raid on some midland city, dumped its unused bombs on my ship, the *Jonathan Holt*, which was clearly visible from the ten thousand or so feet at which it was flying. The bomb-aimer's accuracy was nearly perfect: the two bombs straddled our ship at about twenty yards on either side. They gave the ship and its occupants a severe shock and a better understanding of the phrase 'shiver my timbers', but once again our luck was in and we escaped with only minor damage. (My former shipmates on the *Saint Rosario* were not so fortunate. They were bombed, gunned and badly damaged by German aircraft north of

Scotland, though happily the ship made it back to port and after repairs returned to service.)

After this single excursion I returned to the Saint Line, which had treated me well and seemed pleased to have me back. But before returning I sat for and passed my First Mate's certificate, which brought me a much-prized promotion. The Second Mate of a merchant ship, which I now became, is always the navigating officer. The Master and Chief Officer will get involved with navigation from time to time, especially in adverse conditions, but primary responsibility lies with the Second Mate, who spends a great deal of time on it both on and off watch. I enjoyed the responsibility – and the intellectual stimulus – the post brought with it.

Traditionally, the Second Mate takes the middle watch at sea – that is, noon to 4 p.m. and midnight to 4 a.m. At first it was strange to retire to one's bunk twice a night, turning in at, say, 9 p.m. and then again at 4.30 in the morning. For a while it was hard to get a decent night's sleep from these two periods of rest but the human body is adaptable and before long I regarded the routine as a perfectly normal way of life. I found the time I spent as Second Mate on my new ship both stimulating and fulfilling.

My new ship, the *Samoresby*, was a Liberty ship – one of well over a hundred built in the USA and made available to the British government under the Lend-Lease Agreement. The original design for these ships came from Thompsons of Sunderland (the yard which had built the *Saint Essylt*) and was modified by the US Maritime Commission in order to speed up construction. Liberty ships had a designed life of just five years, though the *Samoresby* lasted for sixteen before being scrapped and many others did the same. Using construction techniques pioneered by the Californian shipbuilder Henry Kaiser, the ships were built in assembly-line mode from prefabricated sections, joined together by welding rather than the traditional riveting. In the early days there were tales of Liberty ships breaking up in stormy seas but in the twenty months I spent on board the *Samoresby* we never had the slightest ground for lack of confidence in her ability to withstand even the most severe weather. Liberty ships were a triumph of Anglo-American engineering skills and played a not insignificant part in the Allied victory.

The *Samoresby* had been built – in forty-one days from start to finish – in Portland, Maine and the Saint Line, as the government-appointed managers of the ship, assembled a crew to collect her. We travelled out from Liverpool to New York in style. The *Queen Mary*, built on the Clyde in 1936 as the world's grandest passenger ship, was at this time (April 1944) operating something like a shuttle service to bring American troops to Europe for D-Day and its aftermath. On the eastbound crossing the ship was evidently so full that the kitchens could only provide the troops with two meals a day. Our experience, going westwards, with a relative handful of other people travelling on the ship, was the exact reverse. One of my shipmates and

I shared a cabin which on the eastbound journey would have had fourteen occupants and the public rooms were almost empty. The crossing, in which the *Queen Mary* sailed independently – her speed providing her protection against U-boats – was uneventful and we made our way to Portland as soon as we disembarked.

After taking over the ship and making some test runs to check on various pieces of equipment, our first port of call was New York, where we were to load ammunition in a dock on the New Jersey side of the Hudson River. Great precautions were naturally taken to avoid an explosion in such a densely populated area and those of us who smoked – as we almost all did then – were obliged to walk to a protected building some way from the dock when we wanted to indulge our craving. We remembered this wryly when we got to Naples, where the ammunition was unloaded by British soldiers who happily lit up while sitting on the packing cases that contained it.

Our voyage passed without incident. By the time we were fully loaded and ready to join our eastbound convoy from Halifax we had a palpable feeling that the tide of war was beginning to turn. Although we didn't know it at the time, it is now clear that, with the occupation of Iceland and the Azores and the arrival of long-range aircraft to close the Atlantic 'air-gap' – and above all with the greatly increased flow of intelligence about U-boats' movements from Bletchley Park (in which the skill and courage of Roy

Macnab's shipmates on HMS *Petard* played a major part)[17] – victory over the wolf packs had been achieved. Roskill records that whereas in the single month of March 1943 108 Allied ships were lost to U-boats, in the last quarter of the same year the monthly average dropped to seventeen, while the Germans lost sixty-two U-boats.[18] By the spring of 1944 it was not unusual for North Atlantic convoys to make the crossing without suffering any losses at all.

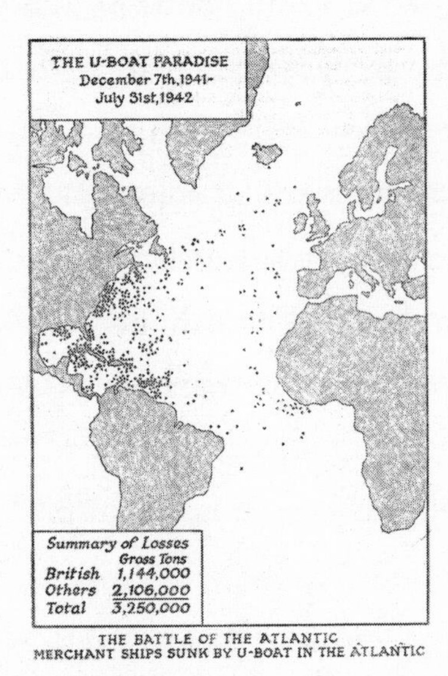

THE BATTLE OF THE ATLANTIC
MERCHANT SHIPS SUNK BY U-BOAT IN THE ATLANTIC

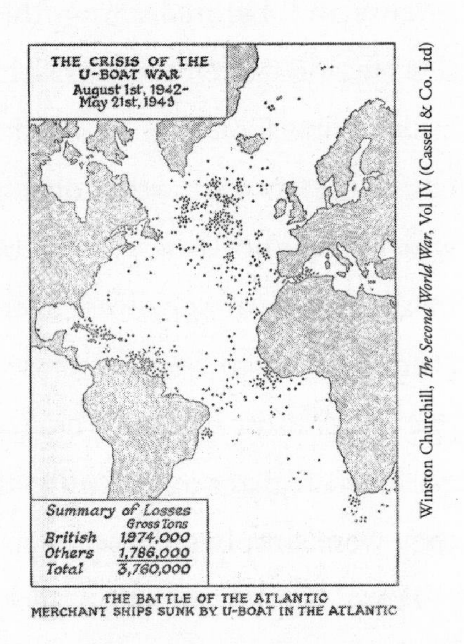

THE BATTLE OF THE ATLANTIC
MERCHANT SHIPS SUNK BY U-BOAT IN THE ATLANTIC

Winston Churchill, *The Second World War*, Vol IV (Cassell & Co. Ltd)

Although no official figures were published at the time, we were all somehow aware of the changed situation. This feeling was reinforced by a peaceful passage through the Straits of Gibraltar and by setting foot on European soil for the first time since September 1939. On the way we passed close

17 See Chapter 3

18 Roskill, *The War at Sea*, Vol. 3, HMSO, 1972

by the resting places of two of our sister ships: first, my well-loved *Saint Essylt*, which had been torpedoed and sunk with over 300 troops on board on their way to Sicily, and later the *Saint Merriel*, which was destroyed while unloading her cargo in the Algerian port of Bone. By the time we reached our destination the Normandy landings had taken place and a new chapter of the war had begun.

Naples itself seemed a sad place. Allied bombing had been intense and, before leaving, the Germans had destroyed the sewage and water systems. There was typhus in the overcrowded back streets and black marketing was rampant. We had some contact with local people and, by some means which I cannot now remember, I found myself involved in a number of social engagements in Italian homes. But there seemed to be no *joie de vivre* in the liberated city. I guess that most Italians were too bewildered at the course of events to register any strong emotions; so far as I could tell they were simply relieved to have survived.

From Naples we went back to London where, while I took some home leave, the *Samoresby* loaded cargo for our next trip. A week or so before Christmas, which we celebrated in Scotland in the lovely but at that time of year rather desolate Loch Ewe, where North Atlantic convoys now assembled, we set sail for the West Indian island of Trinidad to discharge the supplies we had brought from England. Then on to New York where we learned that we were to go to the Middle East to take part in a preparatory exercise for the campaign to reoccupy Burma, which would be launched when circumstances permitted. In the event the British landings took place unopposed at the time of the Japanese surrender, without the *Samoresby*'s participation. Our voyage was, however, for me marked by an almost unbelievable coincidence when, on our arrival in the Bitter Lakes of the Suez Canal, a Royal Navy landing craft was hoisted aboard the *Samoresby*. To my astonishment and delight the skipper of the landing craft, which had just completed what must have been a fairly hairy voyage from Liverpool, turned out to be Neil Bruce, my closest friend at Balliol, future best man at my wedding and now a Lieutenant RNVR. Later that day I made my way to the semi-desert encampment where Neil and his crew were billeted and spent a convivial evening with him. I have no idea how I got back to my ship.

The visit to New York that preceded this was the last of three visits I paid to the city during the war. For me, as for so many visitors, it was a source of endless fascination – made more so at the time by the contrast between blacked-out Piccadilly Circus and the dazzling lights of Times Square – and I have always felt at home there. This visit was in April 1945 when New York arguably reached its apogee under the mayoralty of the charismatic Fiorello La Guardia. In the afternoon of Thursday 12 April 1945 I was on the bridge of the *Samoresby* when I heard the first announcement of the news of Franklin Roosevelt's death on the radio. For my generation he had always been the dominant political figure in the world – long before his wartime activities, his claim that 'the only thing we have to fear is fear itself' was imprinted in our memory. I like to think that the *Samoresby*'s red ensign was lowered to half-mast before any other ship's in New York – as my personal salute to someone who has a good claim to be the twentieth century's greatest man.

By now, with VE Day less than a month away, the war in Europe was nearly over. I remained in the Merchant Navy for another six months but as the *Samoresby* was not required for operations in Burma, my war was effectively at an end.

I have already referred to the phenomenal good luck that I experienced during the war. During my six years at sea I took part in many Atlantic convoys which came under attack from U-boats, sailed either in convoy or independently in the Mediterranean, the Indian Ocean and the South Pacific (though not in the Russian Arctic) and ran the gauntlet of British coastal waters without, as the saying is, getting my feet wet. Having lived to be ninety-five, I am acutely conscious that many of my fellow mariners were not so lucky as I was – over 30,000 were killed in the war, proportionately about the same as in Bomber Command. As a mark of respect for them, I have reproduced in Appendix II a vivid account by Cadet R. H. Davis (my opposite number in our sister ship *Saint Elwyn* and one of sixteen survivors out of his ship's company of forty-three) of what it feels like when your ship sinks under you.

–CHAPTER FIVE–

A BEGINNER IN WHITEHALL

IT IS HARD to describe the feeling of exaltation that I, like countless others round the world, experienced on 15 August 1945, the day the war ended with the Japanese surrender. It was almost too great to be contained. I was on board my ship in the inland port of Rosario in Argentina, where we were loading canned meat and other foodstuffs to take back to Britain. I was officer of the watch that night and so couldn't go ashore to celebrate. Instead, I spent most of the evening, to the probable irritation of the local populace, sounding the V for Victory sign of three dots and a dash on the ship's foghorn.

Virtually alone on board that night, I thought about my own plans. I knew that I would most likely be able, if I wished, to leave the Merchant Navy fairly soon after the ship's return to Britain: but after six years at sea, during which I had become a professionally qualified ship's officer of reasonable competence, I was quite strongly tempted to stay on for the extra ten months that I would need in order to accumulate enough sea time to take the examination for my Master's certificate. The idea of becoming both a Master Mariner and a Master of Arts had a considerable appeal: but in the end I knew that, since I didn't intend to follow a career in the Merchant Navy, the only sensible course at the age of twenty-six was to come ashore as soon as I was free to do so and go back to Balliol to complete my degree.[19] So this is what I did. I finished the current voyage on the *Samoresby* at Cardiff in October 1945 and received my discharge from the Merchant Navy at the end of the year, a little over six years after I had joined it in Barry docks in November 1939.

Glad though I was to return to a college I liked and admired so much, I knew that I ought to complete my degree as quickly as possible if I was to start earning my living and get my feet on the ladder of whatever career I chose to follow, before (as I then saw it) my arteries began to harden. With so many other things to think about during the war and the inevitable uncertainties involved, I had not given much thought to what I might do after it ended. Like a great many young people of my generation, I was clear that if I survived the war intact, I would want to have a career which involved some kind of public service rather than go into industry or the City. I now believe that it might have been better for the country if more highly educated people of my generation had chosen to follow careers devoted to

19 In 2013 to my great pleasure I was able, by virtue of my First Mate's certificate, to become a member (though not a Freeman) of the Honourable Company of Master Mariners when the Privy Council approved a change in the Company's rules

wealth creation rather than public service or academia. But in 1945 there was no doubt in my mind that I wanted to do a job in which the prime motivating force was some 'pro bono' activity rather than financial profit. I don't think there was anything priggish in this attitude; it was probably due to simple gratitude that one had survived the war.

In choosing a career most young men probably look first to their father as a role model and a source of advice and connections. My father – for whom I had a great affection and, as I grew older, admiration – was a doctor but he had often told me that medicine was not a career he would advise me to follow. At the time I thought this was not seriously intended – it was a family joke that Tom didn't like patients. But in later life I learned the background to his advice.

My father, Thomas Steven McIntosh, had qualified as a doctor – and achieved high academic honours – in Edinburgh in the first decade of the twentieth century, when a medical education in the Scottish capital was widely regarded as the best in the world. In 1912, the year of his marriage to my mother, he started his own general practice in England – putting a brass plate on his front door and waiting for patients to arrive, as was frequently done in those days, but following the outbreak of the First World War a couple of years later, he was called up as an RAMC officer in 1915. After a period of training at Aldershot he was posted to a famous clearing hospital in Boulogne where he and other RAMC captains had the job of receiving and reviewing the daily delivery of wounded soldiers from the trenches. In brief, the doctors' job was to decide which of these severely damaged young men could be treated locally and in due course returned to the front line; which should be sent home to Blighty for more specialised treatment; and which fell into neither of these categories because they would die in a few days' time.

For a gentle and sensitive man like my father this experience (which is brilliantly described in Thomas Keneally's novel *The Daughters of Mars*) was evidently – and unsurprisingly – traumatic. One consequence was that at the end of the war he had no desire to return to general practice or take a post in a civilian hospital. Instead, he opted to pursue a career in public health, where he would not generally have to deal with individual patients.

After some years as Medical Officer of Health in a London borough, my father was in effect headhunted by the Ministry of Health, which he joined in 1930. Being something of an intellectual snob, Tom found working with cultivated men (it was almost entirely men when he joined) in the civil service a great deal more congenial than with borough councillors. He had a successful career in the Ministry, which he manifestly enjoyed, and after retiring from full-time work at sixty-five he was asked to stay on as a part-time adviser on the reconstruction of war-damaged hospitals until he was seventy. (He subsequently took some pride in having, as a member of a team led by the architect Sir Ernest Rock-Carling, arranged for all the beds in the new wing of St Thomas Hospital to have a view of the river Thames.)

I was undoubtedly influenced by my father's experience in Whitehall and his official connections helped me to decide to aim for a civil service career. Not long after I returned to Oxford he took me to see the Permanent Secretary of the Ministry of Health, Dame Evelyn Sharp, who was the first woman to achieve this rank. A strong, not to say dominant personality, Dame Evelyn received me kindly and gave me an encouraging picture of life in the corridors of power, which confirmed the view I had already begun to form that a civil service career offered an attractive prospect for me.

In my pre-war year at Balliol, like so many young people in the 1930s, I had been intensely interested in politics. As I have already mentioned, I had taken an active part in the Oxford Union and in the famous Oxford by-election of October 1938 I had supported Sandy Lindsay, the Master of my own college, when he stood as a non-party anti-Munich candidate against the Conservative Quintin Hogg (with whom, as it happened, I was to work closely for a time after the war). But though I considered myself a left of centre person and in 1945 had cast my vote for Attlee (in Aden, where my ship was when the general election took place), I felt no strong attraction to the Labour party. At the time I was convinced that I would never vote Conservative, though I did in fact do so in both 1959 and 1970, being supportive in the first of Macmillan's 'one nation' philosophy and in the second of Ted Heath's pro-European views. In 1951, 1955 and 1964 I voted Labour: but from 1974 onwards I have always supported the centre party – Liberal, SDP or Liberal Democrat. These centre parties have many weaknesses and I don't by any means always agree with their policies but they more nearly represent my values – and a party's values are perhaps more important than its policies – than either Conservative or Labour, both of which I regard as class-based and fundamentally reactionary. This attitude comes from somewhere deep within me and may be partly derived from my Scottish forebears – most of whom, I would guess, were good Gladstonian liberals.

So I applied in September 1946 to take the civil service exam. This took the form of what can best be described as a series of group conversations with other applicants at a country house belonging to the government. The programme, which was modelled on the system used by the War Office to select young men thought suitable for officer training in World War Two, was designed to test the calibre of returning warriors who had spent many years away from their books and was skilfully led by a mixture of experienced civil servants and academics. It was a far cry from the pre-war examination, for which many applicants spent months preparing themselves at a crammer, but everyone in the group of which I was a member agreed, before the results were known, that it was a fair and intelligent system on which we were content to be judged.

Happily, I passed the test and was told I would be sent to the department of my choice. I knew that I wanted to join one of the economic departments and, with a perhaps unfortunate tendency I have often had to cock a snook at the establishment, I had given the Board of Trade as my first choice and the Treasury (which was even more pre-eminent in Whitehall at that time than it is today) as my second. I'm not sure that this did my subsequent career any great favours, though I finally did a two-year stint as a deputy secretary in the Treasury some twenty-three years later.

The civil service I joined in January 1947 was a robust and self-confident institution – unlike its successor today, which seems to be somewhat demoralised and to have rather lost its way. During the war party politics were suspended; the national objective – to win the war – was clear and uncomplicated by ideological overtones. This is a situation with which Whitehall is entirely comfortable and would, at heart, like to see permanently in force. Reinforced by eminent outsiders such as William Beveridge and Edwin Plowden,[20] the civil service did a good wartime job and delivered what was required of the civil administration in such matters as health, rationing, the direction of labour, industrial adaptation and, to a degree, post-war planning. Official leadership of the civil service was, so far as I can judge, strong and two of its leading figures – Sir Edward Grigg (later Lord Altrincham) and Sir John Anderson (later Lord Waverley[21]) – became Cabinet ministers. However, it has to be said that six years of having things professionally very much their own way had to a degree inculcated a culture of what the Labour minister Douglas Jay famously described as 'the man in Whitehall knows best', which was not well suited to handling the problems of the immediate post-war years.

It seems possible that some of this culture may have rubbed off on me. Reviewing my 1970s diary *Challenge to Democracy*[22] nearly sixty years later, Roy Hattersley, a former Cabinet minister and deputy leader of the Labour Party, wrote:

---

20 Lord Beveridge was the author of the 1942 report bearing his name which formed the basis of the post-war welfare state. Lord Plowden was an industrialist who served in the wartime Ministry of Aircraft Production and later became chairman of the Atomic Energy Authority

21 He was, as Roy Jenkins put it in one of his books, the only peer so far to take his title from a railway station

22 *Challenge to Democracy: Politics, Trade Union Power and Economic Failure in the 1970s* (Politico's Publishing Ltd., 2006)

> The author – dapper, supremely self-confident and immensely able – was typical of an earlier type of civil servant. It was a time when civil servants, no less than ministers, believed in the power of government in a way which is certainly out of fashion today … McIntosh was one of the gentlemen in Whitehall who knew best.

The Board of Trade (which started life in the seventeenth century as a committee of the Privy Council and has undergone so many confusing and unnecessary name changes since 1963 that I find it hard to remember what it is called today) is a historic department whose political heads have included the future Prime Ministers Lloyd George, Winston Churchill, Ted Heath and Harold Wilson. It has never been regarded as one of the most exciting or glamorous Departments of State but the jobs it gave me were full of interest and variety and launched me on a thirty-year career in government service which, though not free from frustrations and disappointments, had few dull moments.

I was exceptionally lucky in my early years there. When I started as an assistant principal (the lowest form of life in Whitehall's senior ranks) my two immediate superiors were both unusual people with whom it was a pleasure to work. The under-secretary in charge of the division in which I worked was Alix Kilroy, later Dame Alix, known as 'AK' by all her colleagues and as 'Bay' by her family and personal friends. She was one of the first women to join the administrative grade of the civil service (in 1925) and in a wide variety of senior posts she blazed a trail for succeeding generations of women in Whitehall – though, unlike her close friend Evelyn Sharp, she never became a permanent secretary. When I joined the department she was at the top of her game – an attractive, elegant and cultivated 45-year-old, married to Francis Meynell (the founder of Bloomsbury's favourite publisher, the Nonesuch Press), and a thoroughly nice human being. As her young unmarried subordinate I had a respectful tendresse for her and I imagine we were both aware of this.

Between AK and me in the hierarchy there was an assistant secretary, Herbert Andrew, who had started his career as an examiner in the Patent Office and had been promoted to the administrative grade of the civil service on the outbreak of war. Andrew, who rose to be Permanent Secretary of the Education Ministry, had a razor-sharp mind coupled with a modest and unassertive personality. I liked and admired him and was not altogether surprised when, on his retirement, he became ordained as an Anglican priest. Both he and AK ran their organisation with a light touch and were ready to give their juniors as much responsibility as they could handle effectively. So far as I was concerned, it was a happy ship.

The first job I was given was concerned with monopolies, cartels and restrictive business practices. This was a new subject for the Board of Trade with more scope for original thinking than would have been the case with topics the department had been handling for years. Unexpectedly, the remit to frame a policy on these matters and initiate legislation to implement it stemmed from a provision in the Atlantic Charter, signed by Franklin Roosevelt and Winston Churchill in the dark days of 1941 (before the United States had entered the war). The USA, with its deep-seated belief in the virtues of free enterprise, had always taken a tough line on activities designed to limit competition. Unlike the United Kingdom it had well-established legislation in this field, with substantial fines and even jail sentences for those who contravened it. The British establishment, both industrial and political, on the other hand, thought the virtues of competition could be exaggerated and – notably in the 1930s – had a more sympathetic attitude towards cartels, for which the government was from time to time willing to provide legislative protection.

The Americans strongly disagreed with the British approach and took the opportunity to insert a paragraph in the Atlantic Charter asserting the need for a concerted effort to be made to lower trade barriers, *including activities designed to limit competition in world markets* (my italics). Churchill, with other priorities in mind at the time, acquiesced in this – hence the Board of Trade's remit, with which I, as a neophyte administrator, became involved.

The approach the wartime coalition decided to adopt in Britain, which was reaffirmed by the Attlee government of 1945, was as so often less black and white and more pragmatic than that favoured by the Americans. By the time I arrived on the scene it had been decided that a new organisation should be established to review individual instances of anti-competitive behaviour and pass judgement on their merits or demerits. It was to be the task of the small team led by AK and Andrew, of which I was part, to develop this concept and prepare the legislative and organisational measures needed to put it into effect.

I found this work intensely interesting. Although the most junior member of the team I was the only one employed full time on this project which meant that I was involved in every aspect of the work. I particularly enjoyed taking part in the many discussions the team had with Parliamentary Counsel. This was an official whom even the most senior civil servants regarded with a degree of awe, because his word in matters of legislation was literally law. Sir John Rowlatt, the Parliamentary Counsel at the time, was a man of subtle intellect, great charm and a degree of eccentricity which I sometimes thought was at least partly contrived. When he arrived for work – often a few minutes late, so that we were already assembled in his meeting room when he joined us – the first thing he did was to change the jacket of his well-tailored suit for a shabby black coat of less expensive material. His next move was to adjust the prosthetic lower leg which was a legacy of his service in the 1914–18 war. It seemed to me that these adjustments became more frequent whenever our team began to press its point of view to a degree which Sir John considered tiresome; it is certainly true that we sometimes found it difficult to sustain our arguments when his concentration seemed wholly given up to this ungainly piece of metal.

I got on well with him. His job was to convert our ideas, which were often loosely or clumsily expressed, into words whose meaning was so precise that they left no room for ambiguity or subsequent challenge. This process was so like the translation of Keats or Shakespeare into Latin verse on which I and my fellow sixth-formers had somewhat purposelessly excelled at Charterhouse that I quickly felt at ease with it. This bore fruit beyond my expectations in one discussion with Sir John about the determination by the proposed Monopolies Commission of whether a company's behaviour in any given case was or was not in the public interest. We wanted the legislation to contain some words defining the public interest in cases of this sort but Sir John told us that it was impossible to define in law so vague and general a concept. I, with youthful brashness, demurred and said I thought it was quite easy, whereupon Sir John asked me to write my proposal down on paper. When I sent it to him after the meeting he accepted it without alteration and incorporated it in the Bill he was drafting, which in due course became an Act of Parliament – a small piece of immortality of a sort.

The legislative ins and outs of policy on monopolies and cartels may not strike everyone as intensely gripping but my comparative expertise in this subject gave me one of the most agreeable experiences of my civil service career. In 1948, as part of its planning for a brave new post-war world, the United Nations convened a large international conference in Havana with a remit to draw up a charter on world trade which was to include a section on international cartels. The conference, which led to the long-lasting General Agreement on Tariffs and Trade (GATT), was of major importance to the United Kingdom which fielded a strong delegation. This included AK who was to deal with the section on cartels, with me as her assistant: but she soon fell ill and I was left to hold the fort. Referring to this in her memoirs she says with characteristic generosity that 'it was fortunate that Ronald McIntosh, the assistant principal who came with me, was much abler than his rank would have suggested … and was well able to inherit the UK chair from me'.[23] This of course transformed my role at the conference and cannot be said to have done any harm to British interests as the Havana Charter on which we worked so hard was never subsequently ratified. It was an experience from which I greatly profited.

This was my first international conference and as the section on cartels took up only a small proportion of its time, I was able to observe at first hand the way such bodies

23 Alix Meynell, *Public Servant, Private Woman* (Victor Gollancz, 1988)

functioned – in particular the interplay between the different national delegations and the leading figures in them. The leader of the UK delegation, Sir Stephen Holmes, a top official from the Board of Trade (and later UK High Commissioner in Australia) carried a lot of weight in the conference through his urbane and common sense approach and his easy use of humour to relax tensions over controversial subjects. Outside the conference he was good company and one instance of his sense of humour gave me particular pleasure. It was the custom for the best restaurants in Havana to ask important customers to sign a visitors' book giving brief details of who they were and where they came from; these details would be published in Havana's English language newspaper the following day. One morning, after the conference had been running for several weeks and Sir Stephen had perhaps dined particularly well the previous evening, I was delighted to read that 'among those seen dining at the Excelsior last night was the late Mr W. G. Grace of Surrey, England'.

Unusually, the conference lasted for over two months, which proved a sore trial for some senior members of the delegation who had wives and families at home. For a young bachelor like me, however, it was a highly interesting way of spending time in an exotic country, at a good hotel with all expenses paid. As always at such gatherings, one spent virtually all one's time in the conference bubble and had little or no contact with ordinary Cubans, but I had enough free time to get to know Havana well, to acquire a taste for iced daiquiris and Montecristo cigars and to see the faded glories of the former Spanish city.

This was, of course, before Fidel Castro's arrival on the scene and Che Guevara was no more than a twinkle in a revolutionary's eyes. Cuba was in a strange period of limbo between a military regime led by a former army sergeant named Batista, which had ended in 1944, and the brutal dictatorship under the same Batista which began ten years later. When I was there the country had returned to democratic rule and a degree of prosperity but violence and corruption were on the increase and even to an outsider it was apparent that the situation was fragile. The capital city was a mixture of elegance and shabbiness and, as we walked around it on New Year's Eve of 1948, the atmosphere of decay and uncertainty was palpable. As if to emphasise this, the geopolitical changes which, with the advent of the Cold War, were taking place at this time affected our conference directly when, half way through it, the Czechoslovak delegation abruptly departed and was replaced two days later by one appointed by the Communist regime which had just taken power in Prague.

–CHAPTER SIX–

THE MARSHALL PLAN

THE MARSHALL PLAN was a seminal event in twentieth-century history. It was proposed by the US Secretary of State George Marshall in June 1947 and launched a year later. In the words of Paul Hoffman, the head of the agency which was to implement the Plan, its underlying purpose was 'to help the free nations of the world to get back on their own feet after the devastation of the war and to free them of the need for extra-ordinary outside assistance'. By the end of the four-year period that was set for it, the Plan had gone a long way towards achieving this.

The vision behind the Plan was a very American one. In its belief that Europe's devastated economies could be quickly restored to vitality by the combination of American money and European determination, it reflected the best of America's traditional 'can do' attitude. It also represented enlightened self-interest, since in Hoffman's words 'Europe's economic strength is vital to the safety of the USA'; and as post-war relations between the United States and the Soviet Union began to deteriorate, it offered a bulwark against the spread of Communism. It was also, in my opinion, a noble vision that reflected General Marshall's own idealism – and, I feel sure, his strong personal desire to give a helping hand to European countries that had suffered so much from the damage necessarily inflicted by the forces under his command.[24] It was, one has to remember, a time of great idealism of a kind which has become a lot less common in international affairs in the twenty-first century.

The Dollar Exports Board (DEB), to which I was posted not long after I got back from Havana, stemmed directly from the Marshall Plan. One of its principal aims was to help participating countries to earn more dollars, mainly through increased exports to the USA. This applied particularly to the United Kingdom, which had a larger trade deficit with the dollar area than any other European country. Britain was a big importer from the USA and Canada but traditionally exported the bulk of its own manufactured goods to sterling area markets in the empire and very little to North America.

The Dollar Exports Board, which opened for business in May 1948, was to be the British government's chosen instrument for redressing this imbalance. It was not, however, to be a government department but a free-standing organisation, set up by the Federation of British Industries and the National Union of Manufacturers (forerunners of the

24 Marshall was the USA's top General throughout World War Two and was awarded the Nobel Peace Prize in 1953

present-day CBI), the Chambers of Commerce, the City of London and the Trades Union Congress, and financed partly by them and partly by the government. The Dollar Exports Board was to consist of a number of leading businessmen with a small administrative team to support it. I was to be in charge of this team and, in order to emphasise that it was not a government department, I would be called its general manager rather than its secretary. It was a great job for a 29-year-old – and, as things turned out, a useful dummy run for my final years in the public service, when I was Director General of Neddy.

The first chairman of the DEB, Sir Graham Cunningham, was a prominent industrialist who was chairman and chief executive of a large and successful manufacturing company. He had a strong personality and, it has to be said, was not temperamentally well suited to the chairmanship of a public, semi-political body like the DEB. His management style within his own company was said to be distinctly autocratic and, though I think he tried hard, he never seemed comfortable in his role at the DEB, where the lines of responsibility were less clear than those he was used to and persuasion was a more necessary skill than authority. I am sure it was for this reason – and not for the pressure of work that was the public excuse – that, having got the DEB off to a reasonable start, he resigned after only six months in the job.

The board itself was an unwieldy body, with twenty members including the chairman. Some of the directors were ex-officio representatives of the sponsoring organisations but the majority were appointed on their individual merits for their business experience. They were a group of talented men (there were, of course, no women) who gave generously of their time and made a very positive contribution to the DEB's work. Among them they covered a wide spectrum of industry and commerce. Four who stand out in my memory as hard-working and effective members of the board are: Sir Charles Hambro, an active scion of the banking dynasty of that name; Lawrence Heyworth, a director of Unilever who brought a wealth of marketing experience to our work; Sir Percy Lister, the chief executive of R. A. Lister, a well-known engineering company with a successful record as an exporter; and Sir Leonard Paton from Harrison and Crosfield, an internationally respected firm of commodity merchants. These men, who retained their positions in their own companies and gave their services to the DEB free, were a pleasure to work with. They all played a constructive role in furthering the DEB's aims, both by spreading the word within their own business environment and by sharing their knowledge of the practical problems of exporting to North America with their colleagues in the DEB and potential exporters at large.

One of the directors' functions was to act as cheerleaders for the dollar export drive. This was an important role because their fellow businessmen were much more ready to pay attention to what they had to say than they were to listen to exhortations from politicians. The quartet I have mentioned all spent a good deal of time giving talks arranged by trade associations and others outside London, at which they would explain the national importance of increasing our dollar exports and suggest some of the ways in which this might be achieved in the particular industry they were addressing. These meetings and the feedback the directors received from potential exporters were a positive feature of Cunningham's chairmanship.

In particular, they highlighted the difference between the requirements of the sophisticated and competitive market of North America with those of the traditional markets of the empire with which British industry was perhaps over-familiar. Prominent among these was the much greater attention that those attempting to penetrate the North American market must pay to market research, advertising and local stock-holding. This work led quite quickly to significant, tailor-made improvements in the financial assistance offered by ECGD,[25] the government agency responsible for financial aid to exporters. It also led, later on, to the publication of a 'Guide to selling in North America', for which Laurence Heyworth, Bill Edwards of the FBI and I were responsible. This booklet was handsomely produced; it set a new standard of design for official publications and 50,000 copies were sold.

Another DEB priority was to develop active links with opinion-formers in the business communities of the United

25 Export Credits Guarantee Department

States and Canada. Paul Hoffman and his colleagues in the US government had already prepared the ground for us in making the political case for American businessmen to co-operate with the DEB – a foreign agency which some might think was trying to take business away from them. In a speech I heard him deliver in Michigan in 1949, Hoffman made the point that

> Europe must earn – and we must help to allow Europe to earn – more dollars in order to meet its dollar deficit. This is not just a fiscal or a budgetary necessity. It is one of the necessities of healthy, peaceful and prosperous economic relations between Europe and America. Europe does not want to be a receiver any more than we want to be a giver and until Europe is earning its way and until we in the United States, by wise trading relations, permit Europe to earn its way, our economic relations will be plagued by friction, disharmony and danger all the time … Europe must vigorously undertake the task of earning more dollars. The only constructive way for it to meet a dollar deficit is to earn a greater dollar income. The leaders of Europe today know beyond any doubt that they must set about the task as though Europe's very life were at stake.

He went on to say:

> One of the greatest psychological blocks which stand in the way of Europe earning more dollars is their feeling, based on their own

> experience, that there may be little point in trying to earn those dollars because when they succeed in selling us goods, some special interest group in the United States, which does not like competition, will see that these goods are barred out … I have said to the participating countries: instead of worrying about what America will do, concentrate all your energy on getting well under way toward your goals. Give America specific and dramatic proof that you mean business. Urge your manufacturers, large or small, to take a hard, realistic look at the American market. Find out what goods we need. Send us those goods and back them up with imaginative merchandising and advertising. Put forth this kind of effort and you will have America cheering and supporting you. The American people have never yet failed to back up a game fighter and they will back you.

It was stirring stuff – a brave speech of a kind which no one could possibly make in the United States today. It got a positive response from his American audience and, in effect, made our work possible. I made many visits to the United States for the DEB and never encountered any hostility or criticism of what we were trying to do from the scores of American business people I met.

In Canada the response was equally positive. It led to the formation of a Dollar Sterling Trade Board (DSTB) headed up by James Duncan (the chairman of Massey Harris, one of the country's topmost companies), which acted as the DEB's opposite number in Canada and got down to work with a will. Within a short time it launched an exhaustive examination, industry by industry, of the potential for increasing Canadian imports from Britain, and set up a network of business executives in different sectors to give expert advice to British exporters.

My own opposite number on the DSTB was a delightful Canadian, Tony Griffin, who was eight years older than me. Tony had been a wartime destroyer captain in the RCN at a very early age and was a rising star in the Canadian Foreign Service when Duncan poached him for the DSTB. He and his wife Kitty became lasting friends of Doreen's and mine and, although he is now long gone, I have an unusual and endearing memento of him. When working in Ottawa immediately after the war Tony had been the 'caller' (or master of ceremonies) of the square dances held at Government House, whose occupant at the time was Field Marshall Lord Alexander of Tunis. He told me that on a visit she made to Ottawa, while she was still Princess Elizabeth, the Queen had attended one of these dances. She had evidently been much taken with the square dancing and Tony's 'calling' and asked if the music had ever been recorded. It transpired that it had not, so arrangements were made to put a BBC studio in London at Tony's disposal to make a recording: but he said he couldn't do his calling without some dancers to call. Doreen and I were accordingly invited, along with six of his other friends, to join him in the studio and dance to the music provided. Copies of the recording made on this occasion were given

My mother Chrissie at eighteen

My father Tom (on the left) with his parents and brothers

At Brompton Oratory in June 1951

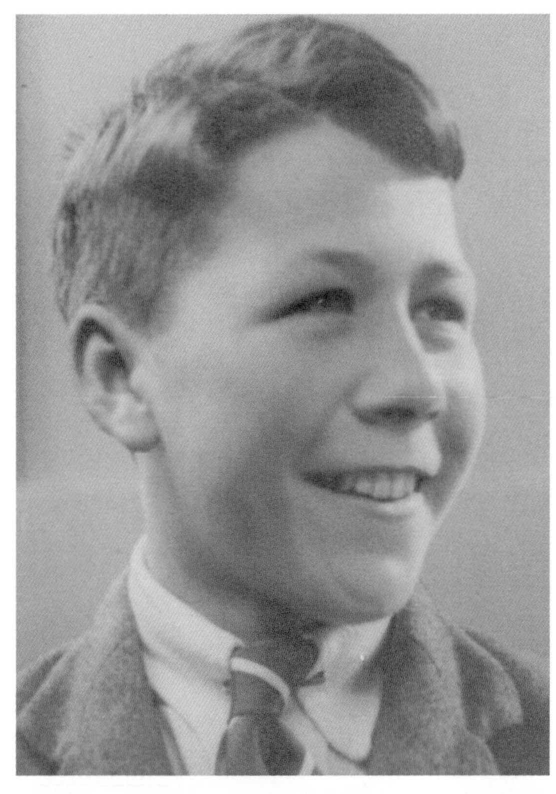

Prep school boy

Robert Birley: his effect on us teenagers was electric

PHOTOGRAPH BY ROGER SMEETON

Charterhouse Chapel, built to honour nearly 700 Old Carthusians killed in 1914–18

DRAWING BY ERIC KENNINGTON

The Garden Quad helped to make Balliol an intrinsically friendly place

My uncle Rae, killed in action near Ypres in 1915

Balliol Hall

The Chancellor welcomes the President to Oxford. Roy Jenkins with Bill Clinton and his daughter Chelsea in 2003

A Balliol quartet fifty years on. L TO R: Roy Jenkins, Ted Heath, Madron Seligman and me

Second Mate in 1944

The *Graf Spee* resting on the bottom of the River Plate three days after the battle in December 1939

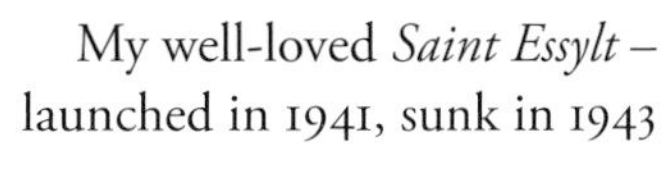

My well-loved *Saint Essylt* –
launched in 1941, sunk in 1943

Dame Alix Meynell

Secretary of State George
Marshall at Harvard in 1947 to
launch the Marshall Plan

Gresham College seminar on Communism in 1930s Britain. L TO R: Professor Nicholas Deakin, Juliet Gardiner, Sir Roderick Floud, Lord (Peter) Hennessy

With my sister Mary and her husband Richard

PHOTO BY ANNA ZEVILLE

Portrait of Doreen by Jane Bond RP NEAC

My great-uncle's yacht *Jenetta* under full sail on the Clyde in 1949

Our yacht *Zeemo* in Calais in 1970

Sailing as it used to be – my forebears in the 1890s

My first meeting with the Indian Prime Minister Pandit Nehru

The High Commissioner's party to welcome us in 1957, with MacMahon on the left, MacDonald in the centre and Midgley on the right

PHOTO BY ANNA ZEVILLE

Doreen's painting of Minnie – a British object by birth

Doreen in the 1960s

to the participants as well as to the Palace and the sound of our footsteps, obediently following Tony's calling, has been preserved for posterity.

The emphasis which those who knew the US market placed on the need for British exporters to adopt an entirely new approach to market research and sales promotion (which were in their infancy in Britain at the time) led the DEB to set up an Advertising Advisory Council. This was chaired by Douglas Saunders, the charismatic and highly professional head of J. Walter Thompson, which was the leading advertising agency of the day. Saunders and his group did a fine job in revolutionising British industry's understanding of the requirements of the US market.

The DEB sent a number of trade missions to the USA, most of which I was a member of. Their task was a combination of salesmanship and learning: the former to make the American business community aware of what different sectors of British industry had to offer and the latter to get to know in more detail the requirements and idiosyncrasies of the particular segment of the US market with which the mission was concerned. These missions were very hard work but also rewarding. I found my own visits to such cities as Chicago, Michigan, Kansas City, Dallas, San Francisco and Denver intensely interesting. The knowledge I acquired of the USA – and to a lesser extent of Canada – during that period became an immensely valuable part of my mental equipment thereafter.

The devaluation of the pound in September 1949 – an earth-shaking event in the Attlee government's life which was greeted with dismay in Britain – gave a big fillip to our work, because it made British exports to North America much more competitive. Within forty-eight hours of the announcement, the DEB issued a 'Statement to Trade Organisations' about the changed situation. This document has a certain historical interest; the following extracts give its flavour – and the flavour of the times.

> Devaluation has changed the look of the dollar export problem – and changed it for the better. Many British businesses will find it easier to sell their goods in the United States and Canada; others will now have their first real chance to enter the North American market with prospects of success.
>
> At the same time devaluation has made the problem doubly urgent. The chances of success are greater, the price of failure heavier. The advantages of devaluation may be temporary – we must take hold of them at once, while we have the chance.
>
> At the very least, we must now earn three times as many dollars by our exports in order to bridge the gap. This is not a pious hope; it is a plain necessity and the measure of the job which must be done, irrespective of devaluation.
>
> Devaluation can help, for it reduces the height of the price and tariff hurdles that have to be surmounted: but in the end the job can be done only by greater efficiency at all levels and the production

of more goods of the right quality and cost. This cannot happen overnight and in the immediate future there will have to be some diversion from other markets. It will not be comfortable or easy but we shall not succeed unless manufacturers, workpeople and politicians put the need to supply dollar markets before everything else.

The Dollar Exports Board believe that the British people have not yet awakened to the meaning of these simple truths. They believe that, in spite of repeated statements, the people as a whole do not yet appreciate the connection between the country's dollar balance and the everyday lives of British men and women.

The Dollar Exports Board are an advisory body. They do not make or sell goods, nor do they have any executive powers. Yet their efforts can be really effective if they have every trade association in the country, every Chamber of Commerce and every Export Group solidly behind them.

The statement went on to detail specific action by government and others which the Board considered essential if the dollar export drive was to succeed; and ended as follows:

Exports of manufactured goods are British industry's responsibility. In the last resort only the management and workers of the individual businesses of Britain can do the job which must be done. Without them the Dollar Exports Board, trade organisations and government itself are powerless. This statement is issued in the confident belief that British industry will respond to the challenge.

Hard on the heels of devaluation, Cunningham resigned and was succeeded by Sir Cecil Weir, a man with an entirely different personality. Weir was a sixty-year-old Scot, who had followed his father in the family firm of leather merchants and was active as a Liberal politician in Glasgow between the wars. He had a reputation as a shrewd businessman with a flair for organisation and had played a leading part in staging the Empire Exhibition of 1938 in Glasgow. In 1939 he was recruited by the Ministry of Supply and from then on he worked in successive jobs at the interface between industry and officialdom. In 1946 he was appointed Economic Adviser to the Control Commission in Germany and after his two years as chairman of the DEB he became head of the UK delegation to the European Coal and Steel Community.

'Wee Cecil', as he was known, had an emollient personality and got on with people of all sorts: I never met anyone who disliked him. By the time he took over the reins at the DEB he was quite a well-known figure and familiar with the corridors of power. As a good communicator with a talent for persuasion he was well able to fulfil one of the board's main functions, which was to raise awareness within industry and commerce of the need for and the requirements of the dollar export drive. In March 1951 we organised a three-day conference at Eastbourne, under his leadership, which was one of the most ambitious ever to be staged at that time. Its objective was to raise the profile of the dollar drive, explain its *raison d'être* and spread as widely as possible throughout the business community the lessons learned about the most effective ways to penetrate the North American market and the organisations which were available, on both sides of the Atlantic, to help newcomers to the scene.

Six hundred delegates attended the conference, which was held in Eastbourne's principal hotel. Three Cabinet ministers (the Chancellor Hugh Gaitskell, the President of the Board of Trade Harold Wilson and the Minister of Supply George Strauss) addressed the conference, as did the Canadian High Commissioner and a tough and experienced American businessman who headed Paul Hoffman's team in London. There were also a number of expert British speakers who addressed the seven groups into which the delegates were divided between the plenary sessions. For me and my minuscule team it was extremely hard work, but there was no doubt that it was a great success and worth all the trouble. Although there are a number of reasons why by the 1960s the United States had become the largest single destination for British exports, I think it is fair to say that the Marshall Plan and the Dollar Exports Board are among the most important.

Not very long after the Eastbourne Conference the DEB was transmogrified into a Dollar Exports Council, with similar objectives but different ownership and organisation. In particular the sponsoring organisations took over from the government financial responsibility for running the organisation and providing the staff. This meant that I and the other civil servants who had been seconded to the DEB returned to Whitehall.

In my new post I continued to work closely with industry but this time I was concerned with only one sector. The cotton textile industry, which was my bailiwick, occupied a special position, both historically and emotionally, in 1950s Britain. Production was concentrated in Lancashire, where many communities depended almost entirely on it for employment, and spinning and weaving cotton were not so much industrial processes as a way of life. In the post-war world this once-great industry, which had up till then dominated world markets, faced an uncertain and problematic future due to the growth of textile manufacture in other continents; this trend had been greatly accelerated by the war and was set to continue, notably in Asian countries where wages were a lot lower than in Britain. Getting to grips with these problems formed an important part of the Board of Trade's responsibilities as the industry, central and local government struggled to deal with the fall-out from the changing pattern of world trade and its consequences for employment in Britain. In those days government intervention in industry to resolve long-term problems was still regarded as a respectable activity by all political parties; my work was full of interest and gave me a useful insight into the state of industry north of Watford.

The head of the textile branch, to whom I and my small team reported, was Bernard Floud, an unusual man whom I quickly came to like and admire. Floud was a sensitive, laid-back person who was very ready to involve his juniors in interesting work and we got on well from the start. I soon also discovered that he had one of the best minds in the department (which in those days, when Whitehall attracted more than its fair share of the available talent, was saying a good deal). I learned on the grapevine that he was one of three fairly senior men in the Board of Trade who had been told that, because they had been members of the Communist Party in the past, they would not progress any further up the departmental career ladder. In Floud's case this meant that he would never be promoted from his existing middle management post to any of the three highest ranks which made up the topmost layer of Whitehall – the equivalent of flag rank in the navy. This information, which Floud and I never spoke about although he must have known I was aware of it, rang a bell with me because both my sister Mary and the man she married, Richard Clark, had also been Communists in the 1930s and '40s.

Communism had never held any attraction for me – as I have already mentioned, my age group tended to have Wilfred Owen rather than Lenin as its guiding light – and curiously enough, when I went to Oxford in 1938 no one ever approached me to see if I wanted to join the party; the only call of that sort I had was from Moral Rearmament (or the Oxford Group as it was known in those days) in which I wasn't interested either. It seems that I was just a year or two too young to be caught up in the enthusiasm for Communism which engulfed those like Mary, Bernard and Richard, who had been born just before the Russian revolution of 1917. All three of them had been at Oxford in the mid-1930s when support for the Republican cause in the Spanish Civil War – a great recruiting sergeant for the CPGB – was at its height. However, like all my contemporaries I followed international politics and was aware for example of the significance of Leon Blum's decision to work with the Communists in his Popular Front government in France in 1936; and through my sister – and, when in 1939 they married, my brother-in-law – I knew a fair amount about British Communists. Although I never wanted to become one myself, I understood pretty well the reasons why so many people of a similar background to my own had made that choice. In particular I knew that my sister, who was born in 1916, had been immensely attracted while still at school by the adventurous new movements in art and architecture in post-revolution Russia and by the marked improvement in the status of women and the official positions they could hold. She had been fifteen when she read (probably in an article by the Webbs[26]) Lincoln Steffens's

26 Sydney and Beatrice Webb, though never Communists, were among the earliest literary admirers of the Soviet Union in Britain

famous remark after a visit to the Soviet Union 'I have seen the future and it works' and she believed him. I am pretty sure that her attachment to Communism owed its origin to an idealistic admiration for the new Russia rather than to the anti-fascist movement of the 1930s – and I don't think she was untypical of her age group in this.

In the period when I worked with him I got to know Bernard well and was greatly saddened by the way the rest of his life unfolded. At some point in the early 1950s he evidently decided that, since his advancement in Whitehall was blocked, he would try his luck in politics. Having stood unsuccessfully as a Labour candidate in the general elections of 1955 and 1959, he was elected MP for Acton in 1964. In 1966 he was re-elected with an increased majority and in due course Harold Wilson considered making him a junior minister. He was then subjected, as part of the security clearance procedure, to a rigorous interrogation by the maverick MI5 man Peter Wright (of *Spycatcher* fame) about his activities as a Communist in pre-war Oxford and later. Not long afterwards, Bernard, whose wife had died at the beginning of 1967, committed suicide. This sequence of events is discussed in the official history of MI5 by Christopher Andrew, who says that 'his family were convinced (probably correctly) that his suicide was the result of a long-term depressive illness'.[27]

I of course know nothing of Floud's activities before I came to work with him in the Board of Trade but in 2009

27 Christopher Andrew, *Defence of the Realm* (Allen Lane, 2009)

I wrote to his son saying that 'when Bernard's problems with the security people became public knowledge I had no doubt that, whatever motivated him to become involved in the events preceding his suicide, he was an honourable man; and that is still my view'. What prompted me to write to his son – by then Sir Roderick Floud, a distinguished academic and Provost of Gresham College – was a letter he had written to *The Times* about MI5's refusal to release his father's file more than twenty years after the Cold War had ended. In the talks that followed our correspondence we both agreed that it was very difficult for the generation born during the Cold War to understand what had attracted so many bright young university-educated men and women, like his father and my sister, to Communism between the wars. It seemed to us that there was an opportunity for a serious historical study of this topic to be made before everyone with direct experience of the period had disappeared.

This was the genesis of a series of lectures and seminars held at Gresham College in 2013 and 2014 with the title 'Middle class recruits to Communism in the 1930s'. These were admirably led by Professor Nicholas Deakin and the speakers included my old Balliol contemporary Denis Healey, who was the only person present besides myself who had actually been at university in the 1930s – and he of course had direct personal experience of being a member of the CPGB at the time. Other speakers were such eminent latter-day historians as Peter Hennessy, Juliet

Gardiner, Kevin Morgan and Geoff Andrews. The seminars attracted considerable interest from a wide variety of people whose parents or other relatives had been Communists at the time, several of whom (including my niece Elizabeth) spoke about their memories and gave their reflections on the people involved. The proceedings of these seminars – including all the speeches and papers delivered and a record of the subsequent discussions – will be included in a book to be published in early 2015, details of which will be available in due course on the Gresham College website.

My hope is that this will shed new light on a historical episode which has been more misunderstood than most; and that it will perhaps convince later generations that the young people who supported Communism in the 1930s were in general neither naive and gullible innocents nor malevolent schemers but responsible adults searching for a way to achieve worthwhile social objectives in the context of their time.

–CHAPTER SEVEN–

SAILING

A CLASSIC 12-METRE YACHT, built in the 1930s entirely of wood, was an aristocrat among sailing boats. My great-uncle Willie owned one and when in 1950 he invited me to join him for a week's cruising on the Clyde I jumped at the chance.

Willie Steven – whose sister Helen was my paternal grandmother, married to the Wee Free minister mentioned in Chapter II – was an impressive person. An intelligent man and a keen sportsman, with a warm personality, he was clearly well liked and respected by his contemporaries. As a male member of the Steven clan in a generation in which most of his ten siblings were girls, he went straight from school into the family firm of ironfounders McDowall, Steven. This had been established in 1834 and became well-known for its innovative designs of ornamental drinking fountains, one of which was embellished by an otter with a fish in its mouth and became a listed building. Between the wars, when conditions in the industry were difficult, my great-uncle played a leading part in putting together twenty-two previously independent, largely family-owned companies to form Allied Ironfounders Ltd.[28] This became a highly successful and well-known British company – not least because it sold the world-famous Aga cooker to so many appreciative customers. Willie was its first chairman from 1929 until 1943 – a job that he evidently did very effectively but which left little time for sailing.

The 12-metre yacht *Jenetta* which he bought in his post-war retirement was designed by Alfred Mylne, the foremost designer of his day. She was built on the Clyde in 1939 for Sir William Burton, a friend and business partner of Sir Thomas Lipton, on whose renowned yacht *Shamrock* he acted as helmsman in the America's Cup races between the wars. The Mylne archive describes *Jenetta* as the greatest 12-metre ever built and a half model of her hull is still on display at the Royal Thames Yacht Club of which Burton, like me, was a member.

Burton died during the Second World War and in 1948 Willie Steven became *Jenetta*'s third owner. By this time he was an elderly widower and had long given up racing at which, as a young man, he had been one of the most successful practitioners on the Clyde. When I sailed in her, *Jenetta* was fitted out for comfortable cruising and had a three-man professional crew. Our cruise down the Clyde, past the Isle of Arran to Tarbert and the Mull of Kintyre still stands out in my memory as one of the most agreeable

28 See Basil Tripp, *Grand Alliance* (Chantry Publications, 1951)

of all my sailing days. Despite the difference in age – Willie was over eighty at the time – we got on very well and I look back on him with affection: but I never sailed with him again. He died two years after our cruise and so did not live to see the resumption of the America's Cup races in 1958, when the 12-metres were chosen to replace the much bigger and more expensive J class boats that competed for the Cup before the war.

After Willie's death *Jenetta* was sold to a Canadian by the name of Curry who – no doubt for easier handling by a small crew – converted her to ketch rig.[29] In 1954 he had her transported on a freighter to Vancouver where, as the largest boat flying the Royal Vancouver Yacht Club's burgee, she remained in the ownership of the Curry family for another twenty years. I myself saw her there in tip-top condition in 1957 when, as related in Chapter 8, I was passing through Vancouver on British government business on my way to Australia. The next I heard of her was in 2012, when by a remarkable coincidence I met an ex-Commodore of the RVYC, Jim Burns, at the home of his relative Tim Young, an old friend and near neighbour of mine in Kent. It transpired that Burns had known *Jenetta* well and from what he told me and information found on the internet by my niece Barbara – herself a seasoned yachtswoman whose experience has included

29 A ketch has two masts and so uses smaller sails, which are easier to hoist and lower than those used on a normal single mast 12-metre

a circumnavigation of Ireland – it has been possible to piece together the extraordinary tale of *Jenetta*'s subsequent history. It seems to me to be sufficiently out of the ordinary to deserve retelling.

After the death of the last sailing member of the Curry family in 1972 *Jenetta* was sold. Following a spell with the sea scouts in Victoria, British Columbia, she evidently changed hands a number of times, suffering the indignity of further alterations on the way, and finally came into the ownership of an unnamed person who allowed her to go to rack and ruin. In 2008, suffering from years of neglect, she foundered and came to rest on the bottom of Pitt Lake – a geological oddity, known as a tidal fjord lake, some distance east of Vancouver. (Remarkably, *Jenetta* was not the first of Willie Steven's yachts to go to a watery grave since, as graphically described in the article from the *Scottish Yachtsman* of 1952 which is reproduced in Appendix III, one of his earlier boats was rammed and sunk by a competitor in a race on the Clyde in the 1890s. Fortunately, on that occasion my great-uncle had the presence of mind to jump aboard the other yacht from which, in the words of the article, 'he watched his own boat make a very graceful and dignified exit to the bottom of the sea'.)

Normally, that would have been the end of the story: but *Jenetta* is no ordinary boat. News of her demise spread within the yachting fraternity and in 2009 – some seventy years after her original launch on the Clyde – her wreck was lifted out of the water and shipped to Europe by an enthusiast who appreciated the value of historic yachts. At the time of writing she is in the German port of Flensburg, in a boatyard which specialises in the restoration of classic yachts and is available to any purchaser with €1.5 million to spend on bringing her back to her former glory. With this history – involving, as it did, transatlantic crossings in both directions on board a freighter – *Jenetta* must, I think, be unique among classic yachts of her size.

Not long after my cruise in *Jenetta* I bought my own first boat – a 26-foot Itchen Ferry Cutter named *Witch*, which I purchased with a legacy from my mother's sister Aunt Dame, a dear person with whom I had enjoyed holidays in Perthshire throughout my boyhood. The *Witch* was sturdy rather than elegant but had a reasonable turn of speed and was easy to handle. I kept her on the river Hamble off Southampton Water but I never got to like the Solent as a weekend sailing area: it was too crowded for my taste and the procession back to one's moorings at 4 o'clock on a Sunday afternoon was not my idea of pleasurable sailing. I was never interested in racing, though I can understand its attraction for others: for me the greatest pleasure that sailing has to offer is to cruise without the use of one's engine from A to B – B being a place one has never visited before.

From this time onwards sailing played an important part in my life, both as a bachelor and subsequently in my life with Doreen. We had two more boats during our sailing career – first, a 21-foot ditch-crawler with a centreboard for use in the shallow waters of the Thames estuary and then, for many years, a 30-foot sloop named *Zeemo* designed by the distinguished Dutch naval architect van der Stadt. His Pionier yachts, of which *Zeemo* was one, had proved their worth when in 1971 Nicolette Milnes-Walker made the first solo transatlantic crossing by a woman in one.[30] The Pionier, which was made of the then relatively new material fibreglass, was an ideal cruising boat – comfortable, easy to handle and with a good turn of speed. We kept her on the Medway (close to Upnor Castle, which was the furthest point in England reached by the Dutch invaders of 1667), on the river Deben in Suffolk and occasionally at Ramsgate. These were all good starting points for cruising either along the English coast or across the Channel to Northern France or Belgium. Over the years we enjoyed many happy cruises to these areas – from time to time in company with our close friends and neighbours Rodney and Pam Sheldon, with whom in later years we shared another Pionier.

As well as spending time in *Zeemo* we made some cruises crewing for friends in other yachts. The most memorable of these was a twelve-day affair in 1967 in the eastern Mediterranean on *Bowstring*, a 43-foot ocean racer belonging

30 See N. Milnes-Walker, *When I Put Out To Sea* (Collins, 1972)

to Noel Bond-Williams, one of the industrial advisers with whom, as recounted in Chapter 10, I was working in the Department of Economic Affairs at the time. Doreen and I joined Noel and his wife in the island of Rhodes, expecting to sail with them and another couple, who were crewing like ourselves, to Piraeus.[31] Noel was a meticulous planner but in the event his plans went very much agley, as the meltemi (a wind not unlike the mistral in the western Mediterranean, but stronger and from the north) set in earlier than he had anticipated. As we were due to sail northwards for the entire passage this was a serious setback – so much so that on some days we were forced to set sail around midnight, when the meltemi tended to lose a lot of its strength.

It was, however, a most enjoyable cruise since after the first few days Noel revised his plan to suit the weather conditions, which had made beating our way to the north distinctly uncomfortable, and we headed west to Milos via a group of lesser-known islands in the Cyclades, which were a delight to visit. Even going westwards the crew had to work hard in the high winds and stormy seas – as I knew from experience, the Mediterranean is not the intrinsically placid sea people often take it for – but this was not the cold, wet English Channel, the sun shone every day and we all had good sea legs. One episode I still remember from this trip was when, after a hard day's sailing, we anchored

31 This cruise is described in Bond-Williams's article in *Roving Commissions* (Royal Cruising Club Press, 1968)

in a sheltered harbour in the island of Astipalaia – which at that time was completely off the beaten track – and I was sent ashore to buy some fish for supper. I found the right shop without difficulty but, no doubt because of the meltemi, they had no fish to offer me and asked if I would like to buy some meat instead. I was then taken to a field close by, shown the available lambs and asked to choose which I would like them to kill for our evening meal. Needless to say, I returned to *Bowstring* with the ingredients needed for a vegetarian supper that night.

Another notable cruise we made on someone else's boat was with our old friends John and Mary Masterman. John, who had been a keen ocean-racer in his earlier days, had recently bought a share in *Griffin*, a fine 50-foot yacht, which had previously belonged for many years to the Royal Ocean Racing Club. John came from a family with a tradition of public service: his grandfather was a naval captain, his father had a distinguished career in the Indian Civil Service, his uncle (the author of the famous World War Two spy-book *The Double-Cross System*) was Provost of Worcester during my post-war sojourn in Oxford and he himself had been a sapper major before going on to be Bursar of Canford School. His great outside interest was sailing and one very good trip we made with John and Mary was from Douarnenez in southern Brittany to Portsmouth via the Alderney race – an interesting experience when wind and tide are coming from the same direction and combine to drive a yacht at twice its normal maximum speed – with a larger than usual, mainly young crew on board. We also made a magical cruise with the Mastermans on our own boat from the Solent to Fowey and back, taking in the delightful west country rivers the Dart, the Helford and the Fal in such perfect summer weather that I think the year must have been 1976. This was the finest summer of my lifetime, which led Doreen and me to hold our June silver wedding party on board a Thames cruiser – a happy and memorable occasion for us both.

–CHAPTER EIGHT–

AUSTRALIA

FRANK LEE, WITH whom I was soon to work closely, was one of the two mandarins I most admired during my civil service career. (The other was Douglas Allen, of whom more in Chapter 12.) In 1951 Frank took over as the top civil servant in the Board of Trade when Sir John Henry Woods – an impressive but somewhat remote veteran of the First World War of whom, as a young newcomer, I had seen little – retired.

Most top officials in Whitehall are able people, who try to do their best for government and country. Their background and training make them good at advising ministers, in clear and logical prose, on the policy options that are available to achieve a given objective. They are often less good at recommending what action needs to be taken to translate the chosen policy into concrete results on the ground. Indeed, because they are so deeply imbued with the constitutional doctrine that officials advise and ministers decide, not a few are disinclined to take any personal responsibility for the practical outcome, which they tend to regard as the politicians' concern.

Lee and Allen did not belong to this conventional mould. They always had their eye on the specific outcome the government wanted to achieve and aimed to give advice that would pass the practical test of implementation in the real world as well as the theoretical test of acceptance in Westminster. In other words, they bore in mind that the object of the exercise was to make something happen.

My experience in Whitehall – and subsequently in the private sector – leads me to believe that British governments need more of this type of permanent secretary than the present system of recruitment and promotion is able to provide. I think it might be a good thing if all high-flyers thought likely to rise to one of the top two rungs on the civil service ladder were routinely given, in their thirties, a two- or three-year spell in a well-managed organisation in the commercial sector – an industrial company, public utility, big retailer, transport or other organisation which has to deliver goods or services in a market economy. I believe that over time this could have a transformative effect on the culture of Whitehall – a culture which all our 21st-century prime ministers seem to have found wanting.

The work that brought me into close contact with Frank Lee was the renegotiation of the existing trade agreement between Britain and Australia. For over twenty years trade relations between the two countries had been governed by the system of Imperial Preference enshrined in the Ottawa Agreements of 1932. This gave goods from the dominions and colonies a 20 to 30 per cent advantage in the British market over similar goods from foreign countries – and even more for some food and raw materials. Imperial Preference, to which the United States strongly objected, had come under considerable strain as a result of the war. In the talks on the Atlantic Charter in 1941 and the negotiations on Lend-Lease the following year, President Roosevelt and his colleagues put heavy pressure on the British government to abide by the principle of non-discrimination in international trade – provoking Maynard Keynes to comment that the US government was treating Britain 'worse than we ourselves have thought it proper to treat the humblest and least responsible Balkan country'. Despite this pressure, at a time when we so badly needed American support in other areas, Churchill made his agreement contingent on the right to honour 'existing commitments', by which he meant Imperial Preference. In 1948 the newly negotiated General Agreement on Tariffs and Trade (GATT) prohibited any extension of Imperial Preference and it was clear that the system could not continue indefinitely. At the same time Australia, whose international security needs had been fundamentally changed by Britain's inability to hold on to Singapore during the war, was looking to strengthen its links with the United States and Asia and to reduce its traditional dependence on trade with the United Kingdom.

This was the geopolitical background to the negotiations between the British and Australian governments, which began in 1955 under the Conservative government elected four years earlier. The Cabinet gave lead responsibility for the negotiations to the Board of Trade; Frank Lee became chairman of a high-powered inter-departmental committee set up to mastermind them; and I was appointed its secretary.

The agreement which resulted from these negotiations in the following year was later overtaken by Britain's growing interest in and finally membership of the European Community (later Union) and its content has long been forgotten – even, largely, by me. I do, however, recall that one of the most sensitive and difficult issues concerned the tariff treatment of the 'soft' wheat which Australia supplied to the British market in competition with the more popular 'hard' wheat exported by Canada and the USA. Fortunately, this and other problems were satisfactorily resolved in the course of the negotiations between the British and Australian delegations, led respectively by Frank Lee and John Crawford, the Secretary of the Department of Commerce and Agriculture in Canberra.

Crawford was an impressive man. A Harvard-educated economist, he spent as much of his career in academia as in the civil service and became a distinguished Vice-Chancellor and then Chancellor of the Australian National University. He and Frank knew one another – though not, I think, well – before the negotiations began and quickly established a close rapport. Frank told me later that they had reached a private agreement before the formal discussions began that, if serious disagreements threatened to derail the negotiations, they would not allow them to break down but would work together to find a compromise which both could accept and would persevere in this until they succeeded.

I am pretty sure that the initiative for this pact came from Frank Lee. He thought that in conducting negotiations between two such close allies as Britain and Australia the crucial thing was to establish a solid basis of trust between the two principals; this certainly proved to be the key to success in these particular negotiations. I learned a useful lesson from Frank's approach and years later successfully adopted it during a sensitive take-over in the private sector.[32] Negotiating tactics can take many forms and an overtly hard-line stance is not, as so many financial practitioners seem to believe in these more macho times, the only way to succeed.

The other Australian personality involved was Crawford's ministerial boss, John McEwen, who on account of his forceful and choleric temperament was widely known as 'Black Jack' McEwen. The long-serving leader of the Country Party[33] and a powerful deputy to the Prime Minister Robert Menzies, McEwen was one of the first Australian politicians to espouse the cause of strengthening trade relations with Asian countries; one of his aims in our negotiations

32 See Chapter 15

33 The Country Party was in coalition with Menzies's Liberals. It represented agricultural and rural interests and changed its name to the National Party in 1982

(which he achieved) was to reach an agreement with Britain that would allow him to reduce tariffs on Japanese goods. McEwen kept closely in touch with his delegation's work in London but left the actual negotiations entirely to Crawford, in whose ability he clearly had great confidence.

The negotiations were fairly complex and lasted for many weeks. I was kept busy recording meetings, chasing other Whitehall departments for their views, drafting papers for Cabinet and keeping all and sundry informed. In due course the official delegations were able to submit an agreed text of a new agreement to their ministers and plans were made for a ceremonial signing by the two Prime Ministers. At that point I paid my first visit to 10 Downing Street, with which I was to become very familiar under successive prime ministers in later years.

The ceremony itself was brief and formal. At sixty-two Bob Menzies was in the prime of his political life and looked every inch the world statesman which he had by then become. He radiated good will but confined himself to platitudes when he spoke. Anthony Eden was correct but detached – or possibly just bored by having to deal with questions of trade. I waited with some interest for his opening remarks in which I naively thought that, with his long experience of foreign affairs, he might throw new light on the project on which I had worked so hard. I was, therefore, a bit taken aback when I realised that, though speaking in a conversational tone, he was reading word for word from the script I had drafted for him the previous day. It was in some ways gratifying that he should do so: but it taught me a lesson that one should never take lightly a request to draft speaking notes for a busy man. It also called to mind the advice I received from an old hand in my early days in Whitehall: 'Always remember to keep briefing papers short and simple for a busy minister; he will read them late in the evening, when he will certainly be tired and may quite possibly be drunk as well.'

After the ceremony the great and the good departed and we lesser fry returned to our desks with the sense of a mission satisfactorily accomplished. For me, the final stage of the saga was a delight. After the signing ceremony the Australians invited Frank Lee to pay them a visit – partly in recognition of all he had done to secure an agreement that was satisfactory to both sides and partly, I believe, to help him to recover from a mild heart attack he had experienced towards the end of the negotiations. Frank arranged for me to accompany him and, being a gentleman, to travel with him in first class. His doctor had advised him to limit the length of each stage of his flight as far as possible to four hours, so we enjoyed a leisurely progress to the southern hemisphere, in stages which allowed for short breaks in Ottawa, Vancouver and Hawaii. On our arrival in Canberra we were hospitably welcomed by the recently appointed High Commissioner Lord Carrington; at thirty-seven he was exactly my own age and our paths crossed pleasantly again when he became a Cabinet minister in Ted Heath's government in the 1970s.

After a few days of business in Canberra Frank stayed on in Australia for a time to help his convalescence, while I returned to England – this time in economy class and with no overnight stops.

–CHAPTER NINE–

INDIA

NOT LONG AFTER I got back from Australia I was offered a post as Commercial Counsellor at the British High Commission in Delhi. The five years I spent there, masquerading as a diplomat, were among the most enjoyable of my career.

During the 1930s India seemed to be constantly in the news. Mahatma Gandhi, the half-naked fakir of Winston Churchill's derogatory phrase, made his first appearance in London in 1931 at the start of an apparently never-ending series of discussions between the British government and India's leaders about the political future of the sub-continent. Though a somewhat controversial figure at the time, Gandhi was widely admired for his integrity and ascetic lifestyle and eventually – and in my view rightly – achieved a status in the popular mind comparable with that of Nelson Mandela seventy years later.

Like most of my contemporaries at school and university, I was strongly in favour of granting India at least domin-ion status – that is, independence of the kind enjoyed by

Australia, Canada and New Zealand under the terms of the Statute of Westminster of 1931. An opportunity to achieve this clearly existed for a short period in 1937; had this been taken, the slaughter that accompanied the grant of complete independence in 1947 – by which time the ambitions of Dr Jinnah and the Muslim League for a separate state of Pakistan had irreversibly strengthened – might well have been avoided. As a keen follower of these events I was pleased and flattered to be asked during my first year at Balliol to give a talk to the Majlis, a political society to which most Indian students belonged. So when the opportunity to work in India came nearly twenty years later I had no hesitation in taking it, with Doreen's complete agreement.

The normal way for officials and their families to travel to new positions in the sub-continent in the 1950s was still by sea and we had a leisurely and agreeable journey to Bombay – via South Africa, because the Suez Canal was still blocked as a result of Anthony Eden's disastrous miscalculation the previous year. I had vivid memories of Bombay, which I had last visited in very different circumstances in 1942 on my way to Singapore. The India we came to in 1957 was of course a very different country. Independence – and the partition of the country into the separate republics of India and Pakistan – had taken place exactly ten years previously and, barring the fact that the commander-in-chief of the Indian Navy was still a British admiral, all traces of imperial rule had disappeared.

Pandit Nehru, though clearly less interested in the details of administration than he had been in his prime, was at the height of his fame as a world statesman and during our time in Delhi received a seemingly endless stream of international visitors, including the Queen, President Eisenhower, Mr Khrushchev and Harold Macmillan. As joint leader, with President Tito, of the non-aligned movement and a friend and admirer of the Soviet Union, Nehru was not universally popular in the West during those Cold War years, but in his own country and in the world at large he was a towering figure. His conservative critics in Britain and elsewhere thought him vain and manipulative, but for me his greatness was never in doubt and in such opportunities as I had in Delhi to observe him at first hand he came across as an inspiring leader and a sensitive human being.

The British High Commissioner under whom I served for most of my time in India was Malcolm MacDonald, the son of the first Labour Prime Minister and, as a National Labour MP, a Cabinet minister in the coalition government of the 1930s. Having been a keen supporter of Neville Chamberlain's appeasement policy he was not given a Cabinet post by Churchill when he became Prime Minister in 1940. Indeed, Malcolm used to tell a story of how he was summoned to No. 10 when Churchill took over. On entering the Cabinet room he found the great man rehearsing the speech he would shortly deliver to an expectant House of Commons: 'I have nothing to offer you but blood, sweat and tears' he intoned – and then without a break: 'I am sending you to Ottawa'.

It was said that Anthony Eden later offered Malcolm the post of High Commissioner in Delhi in the belief that his background and experience would enable him to become personally close to Nehru. If so, he was a disappointment because, as Malcolm himself admitted, the two men never got on well together – possibly because most of Nehru's British friends were mainstream Labour supporters who regarded National Labour MPs as traitors. This aside, Malcolm was a distinguished and respected representative of his country and a delightful man to work for. With his background as a Cabinet minister he was very ready to delegate all but the most important issues to his subordinates, with whom his relations were easy-going and pleasant, and his informality of manner and dress was for most Indians a welcome change from the more formal style of senior British figures under the Raj.

The High Commission over which MacDonald presided was a big one – bigger perhaps than was strictly necessary. To support him he had three men who held the rank of minister: his deputy Arthur Clark (of whom more later) followed by Morrice James (who himself became High Commissioner in 1968 and ended up as Lord St Brides); the Economic Minister Gerald MacMahon, a gentle, teetotal Irish bachelor who was my immediate boss; and George Blaker, a senior Treasury official, to deal with questions of finance. The service attaches included a Brigadier and a Captain RN and the political, economic and information departments were all well-staffed, in many cases by thoroughly competent people on secondment from Whitehall. The two first secretaries who reported to me during my time in Delhi – Peter Preston and Bill Nicol – both rose to permanent secretary rank (and were knighted) at the Overseas Development Administration and the European Commission respectively.

MacDonald was a highly cultivated man of great charm (especially to women) with wide experience in politics and international affairs but totally lacking in self-importance – this made him very good company. Doreen's and my relationship with him and his Canadian wife, Audrey, was easy and enjoyable and they were a popular couple with the host of Indians and others whom they met on Delhi's hyperactive social round.

Independent India under Nehru was by a long way the world's largest democracy and, with occasional lapses, the government and the dominant Congress Party ran the country in accordance with the best Westminster principles. Corruption and political skulduggery were not unknown but in general the standard of conduct and observance of human rights was high during the Nehru years. The administration ushered in by India's 'tryst with destiny' (in Nehru's famous phrase) at midnight on 15 August 1947 was, initially at least, a high-minded one with a strong dose of idealism (though these qualities were less in evidence during the subsequent premiership of Nehru's daughter, Indira Gandhi).

In economic matters the government adopted a more dirigiste approach. Perhaps paradoxically, the high-caste Brahmin, old Harrovian Nehru's close associates in the West all belonged to the political left and his own political outlook was close to what would later be described as Old Labour. As was common among British intellectuals of his generation, he – and many of the officials who served under him – had a great admiration for the Soviet Union and its five-year plans. Post-independence India was as a result a highly regulated country with economic and industrial objectives and priorities laid down by an authoritative Planning Commission. This body was an intellectual power house in which one of the most effective members was an unusual Englishman, Penderel Moon, who became a good friend of mine. Moon was a former ICS[34] officer – a Wykehamist with the customary brains but not the arrogance, whose sharp, independent mind got him into trouble with both his British masters and their Indian successors. By the time we arrived he was a widely respected figure in Delhi and he eventually received a knighthood in Britain.

34 Indian Civil Service

His book *Strangers in India*, published in 1944[35] when he was on compulsory gardening leave after a brush with his British seniors in the ICS, gives an insightful picture of relations between Indians and the Raj in the years leading up to independence, as the following extract, which seems to me to deserve quotation in full, shows:

> In the course of this book there is a good deal of criticism of British actions and policies in India. To some people this may be distasteful. But it is time that Englishmen learnt to view their record more objectively than has been their habit in the past. Criticisms of the British Raj, though often ill-informed and ill-natured, are not on that account ill-founded. The critics may seem unreasonable: but psychologically, if not logically, they usually have some justification; and this ought to be recognised and understood. The customary idealisations of the British Raj are annoying to India, harmful to British interests and quite unnecessary.
>
> For the British achievement has been sufficiently remarkable to require no euphemism or exaggeration. It can stand on its own merits. It was no small thing for a tiny handful of Englishmen to conquer a distant and populous country, to administer it peacefully for over a century with tolerance and humanity and to plant in its somewhat uncongenial soil the great liberal ideals and institutions of England. And no one intimate with India can doubt the admiration and gratitude which successive generations

35 By Faber & Faber

> of Indians have felt for nameless Englishmen who have worked in their midst.
>
> Indians are not unaware of what they owe to England. It is rather Englishmen who are apt to forget what they owe to India – not least how much of their own achievement in India has been dependent on Indian ability and co-operation. Neither the merits nor the defects of the British Raj are attributable solely to the British. Without Indian talent the great fabric of ordered government could never have been sustained without certain qualities – which are also defects – of the Indian character: a respect for authority, a strong sense of personal loyalty and a quick responsiveness to great ideas. The Indian empire is the product of our joint endeavours. Future ages will perhaps admire it.

The plans which emerged from the Planning Commission were enforced by a comprehensive licensing system that applied to most forms of economic activity. This system was administered by an opaque and all-embracing bureaucracy which was thought by some to be a malign legacy of the British Raj, though in truth Indians are more than capable of designing an impenetrable bureaucracy on their own. The system and its accompanying rules were sufficiently complex for some large British companies, such as Shell and ICI, to maintain expatriate staff in Delhi to pilot their visiting colleagues through and around the minefield they presented to the unwary. Smaller companies and others that had less involvement in India could not afford this; it was accordingly an important part of my job to act as a source of informed advice to British companies on how to deal with the bureaucracy and what the prospects of success were in any given case. More generally, I was expected to be well informed about and report back to London on trends and prospective changes in India's economic policy and on how influence might be brought to bear on its policy-makers in ways which would be helpful to British interests.

For my predecessor, Eric Midgley, who after independence seamlessly transferred from the ICS to the British Diplomatic Service and went on to be Commercial Minister in Washington, DC and then Ambassador to Switzerland, this cannot have been a very difficult task. The senior people in the relevant Indian departments were all his former colleagues whose first names and telephone numbers he already knew; and he also had a shrewd idea of what levers of power needed to be pulled to achieve a given result. I had to start from scratch on all of this but had the advantage of having a good knowledge of British industry and commerce and of the leading companies and personalities within it.

The men with whom I had to deal in the corridors of power in independent India were so uncannily like the English public school boys and Oxbridge undergraduates I had grown up with that the learning curve that faced me was not too daunting. India's independence had been willingly granted by the Attlee government just ten years before I arrived; and though the transfer of power had been stained by the brutal killings of partition, the British were not generally blamed for this. My impression was that most Indians were relieved and grateful that they did not have to achieve their freedom by wresting it violently from the British Raj, which, in the event and however late in the day many Indians felt this to be, surrendered power voluntarily. Nothing, they seemed to feel, became their erstwhile rulers so well as the manner of their leaving. This made my dealings with Indian officialdom both agreeable and straightforward; there were only a few among my contacts who enjoyed tweaking the tail of the British lion when I went to see them about some alleged shortcoming of their regulatory system.

From the start Doreen and I were clear that if we were ever going to understand the extraordinary country in which we were living, we would have to take every opportunity we could to spend time out of Delhi and see as much as possible of the rest of India. I was by then a well-travelled man – during the war I had visited five continents in my ship. But living in India was something different, set apart from the rest as it was by its size, its population and its poverty. One of the unexpected things about the country was that you were never alone. If we stopped the car in an apparently empty piece of country and got out to take photographs, for example, there would within five minutes be twenty people or more who had suddenly emerged from nowhere and were watching us intently. There was nothing threatening about them – I don't think we ever felt threatened in India except by importunate beggars – but their attention was concentrated unswervingly on us for as long as we lingered. This took a little getting used to, but the unremitting poverty one saw in rural India was more difficult to come to terms with. We found that we had to grow an extra skin of insensitivity to deal with it – or else it would simply overwhelm us.

Although my job in Delhi kept me very busy, there were always opportunities to travel elsewhere, which I took whenever I could, quite often accompanied by Doreen. In line with its views on state planning and its admiration for the Soviet way of doing things, the Indian government and the Planning Commission greatly favoured the construction of very large plants as a means of accelerating economic development. These included several projects, such as a huge steel plant at Bilhai in central India, which were financed by the Soviet Union. Britain also helped to finance several large projects, including a steel plant at Durgapur in west Bengal and a heavy electrical plant at Bhopal. The benefits these plants brought were probably not in proportion to their size – very large construction plants are usually less efficient than their designers predict and they are almost always plagued by teething troubles, even in the West. They were, however, potent symbols of independent India's new ambitions and were for this reason much cherished by Nehru and his Congress Party.

It was at the launch of the British heavy electrical plant that I had my first meeting with Nehru. Our short conversation at the opening ceremony was not of any moment but I was glad to be able to shake the great man's hand. My second meeting with him was of a different kind. In 1960 Doreen and I were bidden to attend a dinner for about eighteen people given by Nehru in honour of Edwina Mountbatten, who was passing through Delhi on her way to Borneo. Given the close relationship between the host and the principal guest (which according to Countess Mountbatten's biographer was, though almost certainly platonic, an intense love affair) it was not the kind of dinner to which we would have expected to be invited. The French Ambassador and his wife were there and it may be that we were the only relatively senior British diplomats available, but we felt our presence was more probably due to some form of mistaken identity in the Indian protocol office. It was a strange meeting – pleasant and uneventful but in retrospect sad, for two weeks later Edwina Mountbatten was dead.

On a less exalted plane, I was given responsibility in the High Commission for looking after British specialists whose activities were funded by the British government's aid programme. These were a varied and sometimes eccentric bunch of experts whose skills were relevant to India's development and who were themselves often motivated by a strong desire to help people in the poorer rural areas to improve their lives in relatively simple ways. These men often stayed with us when passing through Delhi and we learned from them things about the reality of life in rural India of which we might otherwise never have been aware.

One expert whom I recall was a young ophthalmologist who carried out cataract operations in a mobile caravan-surgery which he took around the countryside, stopping at the major settlements where prospective patients gathered to attend his clinic. I can still remember his excitement when he told us he was now performing in a month the number of operations he would have done in a year in Britain. Another example that comes to mind was the British engineer who had developed an easily transportable pump which would enable groups of Indian cultivators to irrigate their land from nearby streams or other modest sources of water through a technique that foreshadowed those on which the 'green revolution' of farming in northern India was later based. Rather to my surprise I was also given the rather daunting job of chairing a panel, of which the other two members were Indian, to recommend which two Indian citizens (out of a population that then numbered 750 million) should be awarded Rhodes scholarships at Oxford for the following year.

By the 1950s, when we arrived in India, control of many of the British-owned tea estates had passed to indigenous companies or managing agents but some were still run by expatriate British managers. In 1957 the state of Kerala, the region in southwest India to which St Thomas the Apostle supposedly introduced Christianity, elected India's first Communist government. There were still a fair number of British-owned tea estates in Kerala and there was some apprehension that the new state government might pursue an aggressive policy of expropriation of foreign owned land. There was also some concern about the safety of expatriate staff and their families, many of whom lived in isolated places.

As it happened, I had been invited by a British company with interests in both tea and cotton textiles in Kerala to go and see their operations in the state if I ever found myself nearby. With MacMahon's encouragement I took up their offer in order to make a first-hand assessment of how the situation was developing under the new government and hear what changes those on the spot thought likely to occur. As I would be the first representative of the High Commission in Delhi to visit the state since the Communists took over, it was agreed that Doreen should go with me and that we should aim to provide the British tea planters and others who lived and worked in Kerala with a visible assurance that their problems and safety were of concern to the British government. Most unusually but, as I thought, with a sure touch politically, Malcolm MacDonald suggested that when we visited any of the outlying or isolated estates we should fly a Union Jack on the bonnet of our car – a symbol which in normal circumstances would be displayed only by the High Commissioner himself. As things turned out, the Communist-led government in Trivandrum proved fairly moderate in its policies and showed no disposition to make things too difficult for British companies that had invested in the state: but it was clear that our visit and the reassurance it provided was welcomed by the planters and their families, who were in any case a robust breed.

One other piece of extracurricular work I did was my annual attendance at a United Nations conference in Bangkok. This was held under the aegis of the UN's Economic Commission for Asia and the Far East and was not considered important enough to justify sending anyone from London to it. So once a year I hopped off to Thailand to represent Her Majesty's Government at a conference attended by officials from China, India, Pakistan, Japan, the Philippines and Thailand from the region and Australia, France, the Netherlands, the Soviet Union and the USA from outside it. In most years nothing of great moment occurred at these conferences but I still remember the one in 1959, when for the first time the French delegate spoke not just for his own government but for those of the very new Europe of the Six. I have to confess that, committed Europhile that I have since become, I was unimpressed by the French spokesman's enthusiastic propaganda for the new entity.

Outside my day job in Delhi, what taught me most about the sub-continent was the time spent on short holidays that Doreen and I enjoyed away from the capital. On our regular break at Christmas and New Year we always went to Rajasthan, sharing a car with Henry Croom-Johnson, the British Council representative in India, and his wife Jane, with whom we formed a lasting friendship while we were in India together. At this time of year when the sun always shone but there was no great heat, this north Indian state, which had previously consisted of a group of Rajput princely lands, was arguably the most beautiful in the sub-continent. Beginning with Jaipur, which at that time was not the tourist hotspot it has since become, we penetrated further into Rajasthan each year through such splendid cities as Bundi and Udaipur, until in our final year we reached Jaisalmer, a remote town with a haunting beauty situated in the desert on the border with Pakistan. (It was from somewhere near here that in the early days of British expansion in India, Lord Ellen sent his famous telegram consisting of the one Latin word 'peccavi' which he knew his masters would correctly translate as 'I have Sind'.) By the time we got to know the region most princely states were finding it difficult to maintain anything like the glories of their rulers' pre-independence lives: but the process of their absorption into the new India was slow and the flavour of life within them was distinctive and recognisably different from the rest of the country.

We also spent time on our own exploring the lower reaches of the Himalayas in the hinterland of Simla, the old Victorian hill station to which British Viceroys and their colleagues retreated in the hot weather. Simla itself was an interesting historical footnote but the area beyond it opened up vistas of the mountains which were awesome. We made all these journeys driving ourselves in our own car, but almost always accompanied by Babu Lal our gently spoken bearer (head servant). Babu Lal, with three other servants under him, looked after us in Delhi, where we lived in a modern house designed by Le Corbusier (the French architect in charge of planning Chandigar, the new capital of the Indian portion of the partitioned state of Punjab) which was totally unsuited to the city's climate and imperfect air conditioning. Babu Lal's presence was a useful and potentially vital insurance against breakdowns and other emergencies which linguistic and other difficulties made it unlikely we could handle on our own. We enjoyed his company and had the impression that he for his part enjoyed coming with us and enlarging his knowledge of his own country. Beyond Simla we stayed in simple but comfortable bungalows built to accommodate British Forest Officers and their Indian successors in the remote areas we were visiting. Though these excursions never progressed beyond the lower reaches of the Himalayas, they and a holiday we subsequently had in Kashmir gave us some idea of the inhospitable territory in which India's military confrontations with Pakistan and, in our final months, with China took place.

Another important companion on these trips was for a time a black and tan dachshund called Minnie, which belonged to the deputy High Commissioner Arthur Clark and subsequently played an important part in our lives. Minnie, an engaging and determined dog, had been born in India but by the time we got to know her had, through her diplomatic connections, acquired an imposing passport certifying that she was a British object by birth. We looked after her when Clark and his wife were on mid-tour leave in England, became devoted to her and took her over permanently when he was sent as High Commissioner in Cyprus to wrestle with the problems posed by the exile of Archbishop Makarios. At the end of our time in India Minnie returned with us to our home in England where she lived happily and purposefully until the age of sixteen – and was followed in our household, over the years, by seven more members of the same companionable breed. Doreen's painting of Minnie, photographed by my friend and neighbour Anna Zeville, is included in the plate section.

Our official and private travels and the Indian and British friends we made in the course of them and of the busy life we led in Delhi gave us an increasing knowledge of one of the world's most important and fascinating countries. As must be the case with most diplomats in most countries, it took me a full two years to acquire a reasonable understanding of India and its people and I was thankful that my employers had given me a posting to Delhi of five years, instead of the more usual three. This meant that in my last three years I could have some confidence that the insights and predictions I was offering to British companies and others who sought my advice were not too wide of the mark. From the start I was an optimist about India's long-term prospects and I believe that the changes which have occurred in the half century since I worked there have vindicated that judgement.

All in all, the years we spent in India were very important to us both and gave us an enduring interest in and affection for the country and its people.

–CHAPTER TEN–

GEORGE BROWN AND THE DEPARTMENT OF ECONOMIC AFFAIRS

THE GENERAL ELECTION of 1964 was a game-changing event for the country – and, as things turned out, for me as well. The Conservatives had been in power since 1951 and were showing distinct signs of wear and tear. The Profumo scandal, Harold Macmillan's illness and Sir Alec Douglas-Home's weak premiership left the party looking tired and out of date. Labour's narrow but decisive victory came as no surprise and the young, though untried Harold Wilson seemed to many people in and outside politics to be a more appropriate leader for the 1960s than either of his two predecessors.

The Labour Party had done a lot of work in opposition to prepare itself for office, most notably in the field of economic policy. A key decision taken before the election was to set up a new Department of Economic Affairs, which would be 'separate from but equal to' the Treasury. The division of responsibility between the two departments was never precisely defined – an omission which led to endless arguments between them and was one of the key factors in the DEA's ultimate downfall: but the essence of the idea was that the new department would concentrate on economic growth, incomes policy and planning, while the Treasury would retain the traditional functions of a finance ministry, such as interest rates and taxation.

There were various reasons for this decision, which was loosely based on the short-lived Ministry of Economic Affairs presided over by Sir Stafford Cripps in 1947. One was a desire to follow the apparently successful French system of economic planning which had many admirers in Britain. Another was the widespread belief among politicians of both the main parties that an all-powerful and (as many thought) intrinsically negative Treasury was ill-suited to meeting the demands of post-war economic policy-making. A third was the opportunity it offered Harold Wilson to exert some control over his two most powerful rivals in the Labour Party – a skill that he both needed and possessed.

For some or all of these reasons, the idea of the new department was enthusiastically adopted by the incoming Prime Minister and his deputy George Brown, who was to be First Secretary in charge of the DEA; lukewarmly endorsed by James Callaghan, the Chancellor-designate; and vehemently opposed by Douglas Jay, who was to be President of the Board of Trade.

Under arrangements agreed with the Conservative government in advance, Labour scouted around before the election for suitable candidates for the top jobs in the new department. Eric Roll, who was at the time serving as Economic Minister in the British Embassy in Washington, was invited to be the permanent secretary. Eric, who came to play an important part in my life, was born in 1907 to a cultivated Jewish family in Bukovina, an agricultural region in the eastern extremities of the Austro-Hungarian Empire. He came to England in 1925, got a PhD at Birmingham and became a naturalised British citizen in 1931. He was then appointed Professor of Economics at Hull and wrote his *History of Economic Thought*, which became a classic and brought him an international reputation. In 1939 he left for the USA to take up a Rockefeller fellowship but before long the exigencies of war led to him join the British Food Mission in Washington and he never returned to academic life. After the war he made the civil service his career and was closely involved both with the British end of the Marshall Plan and with the unsuccessful negotiations to join the European Community in the early 1960s. In between, he was for a short while Executive Director of the International Sugar Agreement (which sounds to me like one of those jobs which the powers-that-be park you in when they don't know what else to do with you, as happened to me in due course), and in that capacity he stayed with Doreen and me when visiting Delhi in 1958. We both took to him immediately and in later years when I worked under him – first at the DEA and then at Warburgs – I developed a real affection for him.

By then Eric, who was fluent in half a dozen languages, was the complete citizen of the world, but it seemed to me that underneath it all he was the quintessential Viennese – clever, charming, sophisticated and witty. One abiding memory I have of him is from the late 1980s when both of us had long since left government service. On our way home from a visit to China, Doreen and I were in Delhi airport at 3 a.m., waiting for a connecting flight to London, when Eric and his wife Freda appeared in the transit hall on their way to somewhere else. Before long the music coming through the airport tannoy started playing the Blue Danube, whereupon Eric took hold of Doreen's hand and swung her into a waltz in the centre of the hall – something that only a Viennese could carry off successfully at three in the morning.

There are those who think that Roll was not strong enough for the job of permanent secretary of a new department whose remit was unrealistically vague and whose activities were bound to cut across traditional departmental boundaries. Perhaps they are right: it is certainly true that he hated confrontation and was ill-equipped to deal with the rough-house which Whitehall becomes when its vested interests are under threat. But he was an experienced professional with a top quality mind and he handled the coven of prima donnas with whom he was obliged to deal with courtesy and humour.

In addition to Roll's appointment, George Brown conditionally filled two other senior posts before the election: Sir Donald MacDougall, an Oxford economist of distinction, was to be Chief Economic Adviser; and Fred Catherwood, an evangelical managing director of British Aluminium, was to be Chief Industrial Adviser to the department. Both were good appointments.

When these top jobs were filled, Brown looked around for a small number of recruits for lesser posts who came with a personal recommendation from a colleague or a friend. My economics tutor at Balliol, Tommy Balogh, the Hungarian economist who was earmarked to move to No. 10 as Wilson's economic guru if Labour won, evidently put my name forward. This led to a dinner hosted by Roy Jenkins at his Ladbroke Square home at which George could meet me and size me up, with Balogh as the other guest. It was the first time I had met Brown, who came across (as he often did at that time when not under pressure) as an impressive, indeed visionary politician whose ideas made a lot of sense. So, when asked at the end of the evening whether I would be willing to accept a transfer to the DEA, I said that, provided the move was approved by my civil service bosses, I would.

In doing so I was aware that to agree to this unorthodox procedure might be thought by my official superiors to be a breach of the time-honoured rule that civil servants must keep clear of any taint of party politics and so might damage my career – and this indeed proved to be the case. But, as I was not a member or committed supporter of Labour or any other political party, I felt that I could in good conscience accept this opportunity to work in an exciting new department; and as I am temperamentally inclined to believe that interesting opportunities should be taken when offered, I did so. In retrospect I have not regretted this.

Although in the end I lost my respect for him because of his lack of self-control, George Brown was an impressive man when I first went to work for him after Labour won the election. The son of a London van-driver, George left school at fourteen and had no further formal education beyond some week-long courses of the Workers Education Association, including one, I am happy to say, at Balliol. His fellow Gaitskellites used to say, with admiration and perhaps a touch of condescension, that he had the best untrained mind in England.

It was indeed a formidable mind, which could quickly get to the heart of a problem and also had a strong visionary dimension. These qualities – and his ability, when at his best, to persuade all manner of different people to follow his advice instead of their own inclinations – made him an inspirational minister to work for and got the new department off to a very good start.

There was indeed in the early stages of its life a feeling of excitement among those who worked there which I had not previously encountered in Whitehall: one former member of the staff recorded that this applied not just to the senior ranks but to messengers and duplicator operators as well. This was due not simply to Brown's leadership but also to the highly unusual mix of people who worked in the department. In addition to the career civil servants who were seconded to the DEA from elsewhere in Whitehall and generally had a very positive attitude to its work, MacDougall had quickly recruited a strong team of economists, mainly from outside Whitehall, to help in preparing the National Plan, which was to be a central pillar of the DEA's work. But the real innovation was Catherwood's recruitment of a team of youngish but experienced industrialists. This group, with which I had the pleasure of working closely from 1966 onwards, made a big contribution to the department's work and introduced a degree of realism to its industrial policies which is not as common as it should be in Whitehall.

In addition to these initiatives, the department's capabilities were strengthened by a small number of individual specialists, notably the distinguished journalist Samuel Brittan, who brought his original mind to bear on a variety of problems. The resulting mix of personalities and experience made George Brown's DEA a great place to work. I liked and admired him; and Bill Rodgers, who was a junior DEA minister at the time, has recorded that my 'laid-back confidence and innovative mind' made me popular with George.

My own job, under the overall supervision of the deputy secretary Arthur Peterson – a pleasant and able man whose previous Whitehall experience had made him more familiar with prisons than with economics – was to develop a more active regional policy, which the new government had declared its intention to pursue. I had already gained considerable experience in this field under Ted Heath, when in 1963 he acquired, as if in a Gilbert and Sullivan opera, the absurdly elaborate title of Secretary of State for Industry, Trade and Regional Development and President of the Board of Trade. I had also worked on the problems of the North East with Lord Hailsham[36] during his short period as minister with special responsibility for that region.

DEA's remit ran wider because George Brown, as First Secretary of State, had a co-ordinating role running right across Whitehall and covering not only the Board of Trade's traditional function of encouraging the creation of new jobs in the depressed areas but also some important issues to do with transport, planning and office-building which were the responsibility of other government departments and often proved highly contentious. George took a genuine interest in regional policy but we saw relatively little of him, as his

36 The erstwhile MP Quintin Hogg

time was usually completely taken up with urgent issues concerning the National Plan, incomes policy or whatever economic crisis was currently taking place. He consequently left the detailed ministerial work in our area to Bill Rodgers: but he was always interested in and supportive of our work and praised the department's regional work in his memoirs. One happy spin-off of this was the lasting friendship that Doreen and I enjoyed with Bill and his delightful, spirited wife Silvia (who died long before her time in 2006). Bill went on to become Secretary of State for Transport in Jim Callaghan's government and – with Roy Jenkins, Shirley Williams and David Owen – a member of the Gang of Four who founded the SDP in 1981: 'Fourth among equals' as he described himself with characteristic modesty in the title of his memoirs.

Sadly, the early promise of the DEA was not fulfilled. The Labour government's first eighteen months passed without a major economic crisis: but with a big balance of payments deficit, a 4 per cent growth target in the National Plan and the government's declared intention to maintain a fixed exchange rate, the markets thought that sterling was over-valued and that something would have to give. Pressure on sterling greatly intensified in May 1966 as a result of a messy and intractable seamen's strike, led by what Wilson famously described as 'a tightly knit group of politically motivated men'. The government refused to give way to them and the strike ended at the beginning of

July: but by then the markets had lost confidence in the government's handling of the economy and a deep crisis ensued. Wilson stuck to his decision not to devalue the pound and opted instead for a savage dose of deflation – a decision that was hotly debated in Cabinet for five hours but finally endorsed.

The decision to deflate put an end to hopes of achieving anything like the growth rate postulated in the National Plan and has been dubbed by one historian as the day the DEA died. In fact the department continued to exist for almost three further years: but after a melodramatic, on-off resignation George Brown handed over responsibility for it to the Foreign Secretary, Michael Stewart, as the pair swapped jobs.

I remained in the DEA for the eighteen months of Stewart's tenure. I was promoted at about this time to deputy secretary (a crucial event in a senior civil servant's career) and moved away from regional affairs to take lead responsibility for the department's industrial policy. This was for me a rewarding post in which I worked closely with the former steelman Campbell Adamson (who later became a well-regarded Director General of the CBI[37]) and his capable team of industrial advisers. Campbell, who was not only

37 The Confederation of British Industry

an able but also an exceptionally nice-natured man, and his American wife Mimi became close friends of Doreen's and mine – he spoke at my eightieth birthday party not long before his death.

I also had the good fortune at this point in my career to work closely with Harold Lever, the newly-appointed Minister of State in the DEA who had been given responsibility for planning and setting up the Industrial Reorganisation Corporation, which was to be one of the government's flagship institutions in the field of industrial policy. Working with Harold was pure pleasure. He was a wealthy lawyer, with a sharp mind, wide experience in the City, a beautiful wife Diane and a flat in Eaton Square, where he usually held his meetings. He was also Treasurer of Socialist International and had an impeccable Labour Party pedigree, which enabled him to impart home truths about the workings of capitalism to his colleagues and trade union leaders without causing offence. We worked very easily together and were able to get the IRC, which did some good work before Mrs Thatcher abolished it in 1979, off to a good start.

So from a professional point of view my last two years in the department were as interesting and enjoyable as the first two. But with George's departure the light had somehow gone out of the DEA and when Michael Stewart – an intelligent, kind and colourless man – left after less than two years it was time for me to move on.

In 1996 I attended a 'witness seminar' to discuss the reasons why the DEA was created and, more particularly, why it failed. All those attending, who included Jim Callaghan, Eric Roll, Douglas Allen, Fred Catherwood and Alec Cairncross,[38] had been closely involved in one way or another with the DEA and some interesting points emerged from the discussion.

Contrary to my expectation Roll, Allen, Cairncross and Catherwood all thought, in retrospect, that the decision not to devalue in 1964 had been correct. I do not share their view, though I understand why Wilson took the decision.

One or two participants, notably Cairncross, believed that the decision to split the Treasury and create a new department had been a mistake from the start and was doomed to fail. But the majority felt that the decision had not been inherently foolish – it was the way it had been put together that was at fault. I agree with this. Everyone thought that the failure to spell out in detail the respective functions of the DEA and the Treasury had been a serious mistake. But Callaghan added that, whatever arrangements had been made to define the separate roles of the two departments, disputes would have been bound to occur. He had always assumed that if he and the First Secretary had a serious disagreement, the Prime Minister would adjudicate between

38 Head of the Government Economic Service 1964–69

them and take a decision: but Harold Wilson had proved dilatory and indecisive, which increased the turbulence of the financial markets in times of stress. If this was the case, it seems to me that the situation was bound, after a while, to become unworkable.

In retrospect I would add one other thought, which was only hinted at (by Callaghan) during the seminar. As I have said, I liked and admired George Brown while he was at the DEA. He never shouted at me, as he did at some of his colleagues and subordinates, nor did he ever throw a glass ashtray at me as he did at his private secretary, John Burgh. But his erratic behaviour, his drinking and his tantrums were common knowledge and his unstable personality was undoubtedly – and sadly – an important contributory factor in the collapse of the DEA.

–CHAPTER ELEVEN–

RELIGION

MY PATERNAL GRANDFATHER, Robert McIntosh, was an impressive figure, with a long white beard and a large ear trumpet, who looked every inch an Old Testament prophet. He was a Minister of the Free Church of Scotland. For those who are not familiar with the ins and outs of Scottish Presbyterian ecclesiology it may be helpful to explain (as simply as I can) that the Free Church was formed in 1843, when a large number of its adherents broke away from the Church of Scotland to escape from what they saw as state interference. In 1900 the Free Church amalgamated with the United Presbyterian Church of Scotland to form the United Free Church of Scotland: but a hard core of strict Free Church members chose to remain outside this new union (with which they engaged in prolonged litigation) and were known as Wee Frees. So far as I can tell, Robert was part of this minority – it is certainly clear, from all I know of him, that he would have felt at home with them.

In around 1880, straight after taking his university degree, Robert became a Free Church Minister in Alva, a small town at the foot of the lovely Ochil hills in Scotland's smallest county, Clackmannanshire. He remained in that post until he retired to Edinburgh some forty-five years later. My mother sometimes wondered aloud what the churchgoers of Alva had done to deserve this fate.

Robert, who was the only grandparent I knew, the others having died before or shortly after I was born, was by repute a stern figure who took a poor view of human weaknesses. Like all his sect, he had a horror of anything that could be described as even remotely Popish; I was, for example, christened in the drawing room of his house because to baptise an infant in a church might savour too much of Roman ritual. But I understand that he was a good man, of strong Christian conviction, and I have often wondered whether I owe some of the religious (albeit Roman Catholic) faith which has enriched my own life in later years to my stern old forebear from Alva.

Robert's wife, born Helen Primrose Steven, came from a much less rigid and more sophisticated family than he did. The eldest of eleven siblings who were mostly girls, she counted among her brothers-in-law an Anglican Bishop of Oxford and a Professor of Divinity at Edinburgh University. I doubt if she was ever a Wee Free at heart, though as the mother of their three sons and someone who was held in great affection by her relatives, I am sure she was a conscientious minister's wife and a good, if less rigorous, Christian.

My father probably reacted against his own parent's fundamentalist beliefs; for all the time I knew him he was firmly agnostic. While always willing to take his children to church when custom or propriety required it, he was never a churchgoer himself in my lifetime – though, being a Scot, he had a firm moral compass which he did his best to follow throughout his life. My mother's position was essentially agnostic too, though I believe she would have liked to acquire a firm religious faith and, like not a few women of her generation and class, she was attracted to Christian Science between the wars.

In our teenage years my parents took my sister and me to the Anglican church near our London home at regular intervals and were happy for me to be confirmed when the time came. But it is probably fair to say that they saw these activities simply as required features of a conventional upbringing in which they thought their offspring should take part. Perhaps as a consequence, any religious feelings I had as a teenager were superficial; and although all boys at Charterhouse attended the school chapel eight times a week in my day, I rarely if ever attended Balliol chapel when I was at Oxford. Nevertheless, I too have always had a strong belief in the importance of conscience and moral values in human life and (to my surprise and pleasure) was given a distinction for my moral philosophy paper when I sat for my degree in 1947. I no longer recall what I wrote on that occasion but I am sure it reflected the difficulty I have always had in explaining the existence of such human qualities as self-sacrifice and unselfish love if the possibility of a divine origin for them is excluded. As I have grown older, I have found it increasingly hard to see how one can make sense of the world into which we have been born without some form of religious belief.

Comparatively few young people of the twentieth century were actively involved in religion in my youth and, though never an atheist, I was not noticeably different from the rest. This changed when in 1951, at the age of thirty-one, I married Doreen – by far the best and most important thing I have done in my life. Doreen was a 'cradle' Catholic and had a convent education, which can sometimes put a pupil off religion for life. In her school in Harrogate, where she was a boarder, the nuns were evidently liberal, intelligent and understanding women and she left the convent with a firm but undemonstrative faith that remained with her all her life. (At this same school she forged lifelong friendships from the age of seven with two of her peers, Christina de Warlincourt and Elisabeth Royde-Smith, which were very important to her and are still in good repair through my own happy and affectionate relationships with their descendants.)

In 1951 there was still a degree of prejudice against Catholics, from which my own parents and other family members were not immune. This was especially true in Scotland, where the Celtic/Rangers divide was still very much alive. Politically-minded people on the left were also generally anti-Catholic because of the support the Church had given General Franco during the Spanish Civil War. At the same time Catholics themselves tended to live to some extent in their own closed world, mixing largely with friends they had made at Catholic schools or through church and family connections. This was certainly true of Doreen until, when war broke out, she joined the Ministry of Supply and became involved in the wider world. It was also true that I had known very few Catholics until I met her – my girl friends were usually the sisters of boys who had been to Rugby, Marlborough or Westminster rather than Ampleforth, Downside or Stonyhurst.

Things were, however, beginning to change. Novelists and other writers, oddly enough, played an important part in this – Ronald Knox, G. K. Chesterton, Evelyn Waugh, Hilaire Belloc and Graham Greene were all widely read and made many readers aware of Catholicism, generally portrayed in a favourable light, in a way that most of them had never been before. Another factor which helped to break down – and I think one can say virtually eliminate – anti-Catholic attitudes was the change in the Church brought about by the Second Vatican Council. The decision by the charismatic – and now sanctified – Italian Pope John XXIII to call a worldwide Council of Catholic Bishops in 1962, with a remit to achieve what he called the '*aggiornamento*' of their Church, had an impact which went far beyond practising Roman Catholics.

The long-term consequences of Vatican II have been disappointing, due to the lack of enthusiasm – and in many cases outright opposition – of conservative forces in Rome. But though few non-Catholics may now remember this, its effect on the perception of the Church by both its members and people at large was at the time dramatic. Before the Council began, the Roman Curia (the papal civil service, which was conservative to a man) had prepared a voluminous set of documents on all aspects of the Council's agenda: but quite early on in the proceedings the assembled bishops in effect tore these up and agreed new drafts, based on their own views and pastoral experience. This led to a series of revolutionary pronouncements on the liturgy (where the use of Latin in the mass was all but abolished); the governance of the Church (where the principle of collegiality was to be substituted for the previous authoritarian rule); the respective roles of the priesthood and the laity (where deference was to be replaced by mutual respect); and relations with other Christian denominations and with non-Christian religions (including Jews, who were no longer to be anathematised as Jesus's killers). These documents pointed the way to a transformative opening up of the Church to the modern world.

The major factor in my own journey to Catholicism was the fact that from the beginning of our marriage I accompanied Doreen to mass every Sunday – except for occasions when illness or geography made it impossible, I can count on the fingers of one hand the weekends when I have missed mass since we married in 1951. No doubt at the start I went primarily for reasons of companionship, but as I became familiar with the unvarying form and ritual (and in those days language) of the mass – and the lightly-worn discipline which, in the early days at least, made attendance at Sunday mass automatic for all practising Catholics – I became increasingly sympathetic to Catholicism. It was, however, Vatican II and its '*aggiornamento*' which, after twenty years of marriage, made me decide to become a Catholic and to receive communion at mass instead of simply attending as a sympathetic observer – a decision I have never for a moment regretted. It was also Vatican II which made it possible for the Queen to appoint Cardinal Basil Hume, a man she greatly admired, to the Order of Merit shortly before he died – something which would have been inconceivable a generation earlier.

It was Basil Hume – or Uncle George, as his family called him – who received me into the Church. I had got to know him through John Hunt (later Cabinet Secretary and Lord Hunt of Tanworth) whom I first met when we both joined the civil service in 1947. John, who had opted for the Dominions Office, soon married and was posted to Ceylon. A little later I too married and, as related in Chapter 9, was seconded to the British High Commission in Delhi. When we were both back in London in the early 1960s John and I picked up our friendship again and our wives became close friends. John's wife was a great charmer, whose bubbly nature brilliantly complemented her husband's more staid personality. Doreen and I were both very fond of her and became close to the whole family but, alas, she died of cancer at the age of fifty. Some years later John met and married Madeleine Hume, who was by then herself widowed. Though she had quite a different personality from John's first wife, Madeleine too was a lovable person and we quickly became friends not only with her but with her brother, George Basil, as well.

The future Cardinal was a remarkable and very likeable man for whom I had a great admiration. The son of an English doctor and a French Catholic mother, George Basil had become a Benedictine monk on leaving school and Abbot of Ampleforth when he was forty. His unexpected appointment as Archbishop of Westminster and hence leader of the Catholic Church in England and Wales was an inspired choice; and in the twenty-three years he held the post he did a huge amount to bring Catholics into the mainstream of British life and to do away with any remaining prejudice against them.

Hume had a remarkable quality of holiness about him, which was widely recognised by non-believers as well as churchgoers, but he combined this with a completely down to earth approach and was the only man I have known who could quite happily combine a reference to theology and Newcastle United (of which he was a dedicated supporter) in the same sentence. I treasure his response when I phoned him to say that I was pretty sure I wanted to become a Catholic and asked for his advice. As I, doubtless haltingly, explained my reasons, the Archbishop heard me out, reflected for a moment and then said, 'well, if I were you I'd give it a go'; and not long afterwards he received me and my immortal soul into the Church in Westminster Cathedral.

Sadly, Hume died before his time in 1999. John, Madeleine and Doreen are now all gone too and I am the only survivor of the friendship but my position as a kind of honorary member of the Hunt/Hume clan is a great pleasure to me and I am still close to several members of later generations in both branches of the family. To the great regret of myself and many other English Catholics the promise of Vatican II has not been fulfilled. When the fiftieth anniversary of the Council's opening came along, I wanted my own parish in Faversham to mark the occasion in some appropriate way, not least so that those of us who were around at the time could explain to our younger colleagues the sense of excitement and optimism the Council generated. This particular parish is full of intelligent, committed men and women who think for themselves on issues of concern to their church, and is served by an exceptional group of Carmelite Friars with whom it is a pleasure to be associated. I shared my thoughts with Father Wilfrid McGreal, a former parish priest at Faversham who became the top Carmelite (aka Prior-Provincial) in Britain and a dear friend. It turned out that he had been thinking along the same lines and was willing to give a couple of talks on the work of the Council and its conclusions. We accordingly made arrangements to have three Lenten talks about Vatican II, of which Wilfrid gave the first two; the third was given by John Wilkins, a former editor of the respected Catholic periodical *The Tablet* (of which I was for several years a trustee). The title of Wilkins's talk – 'Vatican II: a glass half full or a glass half empty?' – illustrates the feelings that many English Catholics have about the direction the Church has taken in the last half century. Wilkins's verdict, with which I would agree, was that the supporters and opponents of Vatican II in the world church had so far held each other nearly to a draw. Many of us are now increasingly optimistic that Pope Francis's papacy will bring about a return to the spirit of Vatican II.

The success of these first Lenten talks persuaded the parish to make them an annual event and in the following year my adventurous suggestion that the topic should be 'The role of women in the Catholic Church' was adopted.

The talks were organised by a small committee of women parishioners, to which I was co-opted as an honorary member. Wilfrid opened the batting again and was followed by the eminent Catholic theologian Professor Tina Beattie and Canon Clare Edwards from Canterbury Cathedral. The event was well attended by both Catholics and Anglicans and very well received. The general tenor of the talks was, on balance, encouraging to those who want to see changes in the Catholic Church and confirmed my belief that lay Catholics at the grass roots will become increasingly important agents of change in their Church – whether in the role of women, ecumenism or other matters – in the current century.

For me, lack of progress in moves to bring the Anglican and Roman Catholic churches closer together has been especially disappointing. As I move towards the end of my life, I believe that if and when I encounter the Archangel at the gates of heaven, he (or she) will certainly be interested in whether I was a Christian but is unlikely to ask me which particular branch I belonged to. Vatican II's pronouncements on relations between the Christian churches were very positive but, sadly, prolonged inter-denominational discussions on the subject since then have run into the buffers. I don't know where the primary responsibility for this lies – it assuredly does not reflect opinion at the grass roots in England.

In my own community the ecumenical spirit is alive and well. I am glad to say that an initiative of mine has helped in this. The Anglican parish of Throwley, where I live, has a beautiful and historic pre-Reformation church which started life in the twelfth century as the daughter church of an Abbey in St Omer in Picardy. Some years ago I founded the Friends of Throwley Church to raise funds from residents and others of all religions and none – including Catholics, Jews, agnostics and non-believers – in order to help the small congregation to preserve this building as a living church. The local Anglicans then invited my Carmelite friend Father Wilfrid to celebrate an annual mass in Throwley, which is always well attended by both Anglicans and Catholics. When Doreen died the Anglicans asked me if I would like her to be buried in their churchyard opposite my house, where her body now lies, as mine will in due course. In the face of this kind of relationship at grass roots level it is incomprehensible to me that the two hierarchies have made such negligible progress in the attempt to bring their churches closer to one another.

Doreen is also commemorated in Madeira – and is indeed the second member of my family to be so as my father's cousin Ann Welch, the daughter of the Professor of Divinity mentioned earlier, died while on holiday at there in the 1990s and is buried in the Protestant cemetery in Funchal. Our love affair with this Atlantic island began in 1990 when we paid our first visit there. Like so many British visitors before us, we were captivated by Madeira's beauty, its abundant flowers and perhaps most of all by its friendly people. Its attraction was greatly enhanced by Reid's

Hotel, a famous watering hole on a cliff outside Funchal, which was founded by a Scottish engineer in 1891 and, in terms of all-round customer satisfaction, can reasonably be described as one of the half dozen best hotels in the world. After that visit we went back to the island every winter until Doreen's health made travel impracticable; and since her death in 2009 I have visited it two or three times a year.

Somewhat surprisingly Funchal, the only town of any size on the island, is Portugal's third city after Lisbon and Oporto. It has a cathedral, a university college and a fine conservatoire of music and supports a cultural life far superior to most tourist resorts – with a charming late nineteenth-century municipal theatre (reminiscent of many in the Austro-Hungarian Empire, whose last Emperor is, as it happens, buried in Madeira) among its many notable buildings. Portugal is a strongly Catholic country and an English-language mass is held every Sunday in a seventeenth-century chapel of great beauty a few hundred yards from the ocean. Celebrated by my good friend Father Bernardino, who is ecumenical to his fingertips, this mass is always well attended, by visitors and permanent residents alike and by Anglicans and Lutherans as well as Catholics. But Portugal's economic difficulties have resulted in the chapel being allowed to fall into disrepair which, if continued for much longer, would be bound to lead to its closure.

In 2013 I was pleased to be able to fund, in Doreen's memory, the restoration of the roof and the water-damaged painted ceiling of the nave which gives the chapel much of its character. This has led to a valued friendship with John Paredes, the architect who supervised the restoration. John, who spent four years studying at the Mackintosh School of Architecture in Glasgow, and his wife Maria live in a lovely town house near the centre of Funchal, which combines elegant living quarters with a historic store-room for the malmsey, bual and sercial Madeira wines the family has been blending for generations. Through John I have been able to see aspects of Madeira's social life which I would not have penetrated as a simple tourist, including a well-attended reception for the Duke of Braganza, the Pretender to Portugal's throne which ceased to exist over a hundred years ago. When the restoration was complete and the splendid ceiling, skilfully repainted by young restorer Jelka Baras, could be seen again in all its glory, John, Jelka and I were interviewed for a cultural programme on local TV about the restoration of the chapel. I left the island the following day and was approached at the airport by a Madeiran lady, who recognised me from the TV programme and wanted to thank me for restoring the chapel in which she had been married twenty years before. This gave me great pleasure and made the whole project seem thoroughly worthwhile.

–CHAPTER TWELVE–

LAST YEARS IN WHITEHALL

IN 1968 I began a two-year assignment to the Cabinet Office. I found this intensely interesting and deeply frustrating in equal measure – interesting because, after a twenty-year apprenticeship, I had now reached the centre of government, and frustrating because I didn't get on with my new boss, Cabinet Secretary Sir Burke Trend.

The Cabinet Office was in those days a small department quite unlike its modern counterpart. It was also unique in not having, as it does today, a ministerial head in charge of day-to-day operations. In terms of accountability to Parliament the Prime Minister was its head: but since its function was – at least in theory – to serve the Cabinet as a whole, this responsibility was more nominal than real and in practice the Cabinet Secretary was the man (so far the post has never been held by a woman) in charge. In my time the Cabinet Secretary was also the Prime Minister's undisputed chief policy adviser, which made him a hugely influential figure throughout the whole apparatus of government.

My appointment was as the deputy secretary with responsibility for economic matters. There were two other deputies – one responsible for foreign policy and defence and the other for non-economic questions of domestic policy. I was very fortunate in having as my Foreign Office colleague Robin Hooper, a fellow Carthusian five years older than me who became a close friend. Robin had had an adventurous war, flying secret agents to rural areas in France in Lysander aircraft, which could land on and normally take off from farm fields. On the last occasion his Lysander didn't manage the take-off for his journey home and he had to find his own way back through Spain to avoid capture and probable execution. He had been chosen for this work partly because of his exceptional fluency in French. Once, when I told him just before a Cabinet meeting that I would soon have to make a speech in French at my niece Priscilla's forthcoming marriage to a Frenchman – she and Michel had met on a ferry from Piraeus to Crete and are now not far short of their golden wedding – he used one of the *longueurs* in the subsequent Cabinet debate to draft an impeccable text for this purpose, while I recorded the discussion.

I was less fortunate in my relationship with the Cabinet Secretary. Trend was a very clever man of the old school, who got a First at Merton (Oxford's oldest college) and joined the civil service in 1936. In marked contrast to his successor, my friend John Hunt, Trend was a famously secretive man, who played his cards very close to his chest and never let you know what he was thinking – not a team player, let alone a team leader. I found him a difficult man to work with and, as I am sure he felt the same about me, our relationship was never close.

As one of his deputies, I attended every Cabinet meeting that had an economic item on its agenda – and in the late 1960s that meant virtually all of them. Relations between Cabinet ministers and senior Cabinet Office officials have usually, I think, been good, and that was certainly the case in my time. I found it stimulating to work with a group of politicians who, whatever their other strengths or weaknesses may have been, had a combined intellectual horsepower to match that of any other twentieth-century Cabinet. I had got to know and like Harold Wilson (a former Oxford don) in my early days in Whitehall, when he was President of the Board of Trade; and though he complicated life for himself by seeing a conspiracy round every corner, I believe his overall performance as Prime Minister is generally underrated nowadays. My Balliol contemporaries, Denis Healey and Roy Jenkins, were both outstanding ministers – the former at Defence and the latter as Chancellor; and Tony Crosland and Richard Crossman, though perhaps less effective in office, both had formidable intellects.

It was through this connection that I got to know George Thomson who, as Commonwealth Secretary, joined the Cabinet not long after I started my new job. As the latest recruit to the Cabinet, George then sat at the lowest end of the table, next to the civil servants like me, and from this unorthodox beginning a lifelong friendship developed. George, a social democrat whose views on most political issues were similar to mine, was an immensely likeable man and as we both had weekend homes in Kent our friendship ripened quickly. Happily, a tradition of joint family celebrations of Hogmanay, which started in our home in Throwley in those far-off days, still continues – despite the deaths of Doreen, George and his effervescent wife Grace – in the hospitable holiday home in Cumbria of his daughter Caroline and her husband Roger (now Lord) Liddle.[39]

One of the most colourful people working in the Cabinet Office in my time was Solly Zuckerman, who served as the government's Chief Scientific Adviser under both Wilson and Heath. Solly was an ebullient South African who had started his career as an expert in the biology of baboons and was something of a polymath. He had given distinguished service during the war as a civilian adviser to Admiral Mountbatten and was Chief Scientific Adviser to the Ministry of Defence in the early 1960s; by the time I got to know him he seemed to be on first name terms with everyone who mattered in both London and Washington. At one of the earliest Cabinet meetings I attended as a new recruit, Solly was put in charge of dealing with the first big oil spill

39 Chief Executive of the English National Ballet and Chairman of Policy Network respectively

to come ashore in the United Kingdom. This occurred when the 120,000-ton tanker the SS *Torrey Canyon* (at that time one of the largest ships afloat) ran, fully loaded, on to a reef off Land's End. The ship had driven so hard on to the rocks that it proved impossible to float or pull her off and after a few days she broke her back, with three fatalities on board. Solly, who had worked closely with the RAF during the war, was asked to find the best way to get rid of the 90,000 tons of oil that was threatening the coast of Cornwall and the Scilly Isles. He recommended setting it alight by bombing the Torrey Canyon. Amid huge press publicity this was done successfully, though only just because the oil failed to catch fire until the last minute.

Harold Wilson had a particular interest in this incident as he had a holiday home in the Scilly Isles. For this, Doreen, who was at the time he bought it working in the Board of Trade, was unexpectedly responsible. In the absence of any of her seniors, she had been summoned to see him, in his early days as President, to explain some point in a departmental paper with which she had been concerned. After this had been dealt with Wilson, in his friendly way, engaged her in conversation and she mentioned that she would shortly be going on holiday in the Scillies. In answer to his enquiries she told Wilson something about the islands' attractions and this led in due course to his purchase of the holiday home in St Mary's Island to which he and his wife Mary became greatly attached.

I found Solly a delightful companion when I wanted to blow off steam about my frustrations in the office. He was fifteen years older than me and one of those rare people who are both good talkers and good listeners. He understood the reasons for my frustration and shared some of them and I always left his room feeling better than when I had arrived.

Another senior colleague of whom I saw a fair bit at this time was Dick White, a legendary figure from the secret world who was, according to the title of his 1995 biography, 'the perfect English spy'.[40] White was the only man to head both the Security Service (MI5) and the Secret Intelligence Service (MI6); when I met him in 1968 he was the newly appointed Intelligence Co-ordinator and first chairman of the Cabinet Committee set up, in the wake of the security debacles associated with Kim Philby and his friends, to oversee the two agencies' work. White was an engaging but by no means overpowering man, who must have owed his hugely successful career partly to the fact that everyone who met him (including me) liked him. As Intelligence Co-ordinator White was based in the Cabinet Office, where I also got to know the heads of the individual intelligence services – occasionally through my work but more often in the Cabinet Office mess, an upmarket canteen, run by an Admiral's widow and open only to those with the requisite security clearance. They were a mixed bunch: the MI5 people often at

40 Tom Bower, *The Perfect English Spy: Sir Dick White and the Secret War* (London: Heinemann, 1995)

that time former Indian policemen – the MI6 men usually cleverer but perhaps not always such stable personalities.

Despite my periodic bouts of frustration, I found the work interesting. In addition to attending Cabinet and Cabinet Committee meetings and briefing the Prime Minister or Committee chairman for them, Cabinet Office staff often had to co-ordinate Whitehall's work on subjects that cut across departmental boundaries. Through this I got to know my opposite numbers in all the economic departments, which stood me in good stead in my remaining years in Whitehall, when I became immersed in the task of co-ordinating the Heath government's attempts to control inflation through incomes policy.

Aged fifty, with over twenty years of varied service in a number of departments behind me, I felt – hopefully without undue conceit – that I was reasonably well qualified for promotion to permanent secretary, but the powers-that-be thought otherwise. As my two-year stint at the Cabinet Office drew to a close, I was summoned by William Armstrong, the Head of the Civil Service, to be told what was in store for me.

Armstrong was a strange man. After taking his degree at Oxford he joined the civil service in 1938 but, after five years at the Board of Education, someone clearly spotted his potential as he was transferred from what in wartime must have been a very unexciting job to be private secretary to the Cabinet Secretary, Edward Bridges. For a 28-year-old principal this was about the most prestigious post in Whitehall and Armstrong never looked back. Leaving the Cabinet Office in 1945, he was appointed Principal Private Secretary to three Chancellors of the Exchequer in succession (Cripps, Gaitskell and Rab Butler) before rising seamlessly to be Permanent Secretary of the Treasury in 1962 and Head of the Civil Service in 1968. During that time he showed himself to be a formidably efficient administrator who could present to ministers the policy options available to them with great lucidity, but as with my erstwhile colleague Burke Trend nobody ever knew – until he reached the very top – what his own opinions on these options were. As Permanent Secretary of the Treasury he became more ready to make firm recommendations but, as I have recorded in *Challenge to Democracy*, Roy Jenkins told me that, when he became Chancellor after the devaluation of November 1967, the advice Armstrong gave him was thoroughly bad. Roy himself had wanted to introduce an emergency budget in January 1968, with an increase in taxation to control the post-devaluation spending spree, but Armstrong had dissuaded him and our economic problems had been much harder to deal with as a result.

When the Conservatives came to power after the general election of June 1970, Armstrong as Head of the Civil Service (a non-job which left him plenty of spare time) became so close to Ted Heath that some journalists dubbed him 'the deputy Prime Minister'. In 1974 he had a spectacular mental breakdown which ended his civil service career – though it did not prevent him from later becoming chairman of the Midland Bank.

When I saw him in January 1970 Armstrong told me that I would not be promoted to permanent secretary because I was considered 'too political'. I assumed that this was a reference to George Brown's personal request for me to join the DEA in 1964 – and to a subsequent request for my services from Barbara Castle, then Minister of Transport, which I declined. I thought it ironic that, as someone who had deliberately avoided any allegiance to a political party, I should be categorised in this way, but I had foreseen trouble at the introductory dinner Roy Jenkins gave for George and me before the 1964 election. If, on the other hand, he meant that I was a political (with a small p) animal rather than a bureaucratic one, he was probably right. In any case I had to accept the situation as it was; there was no right of appeal. In the event I continued as a deputy secretary for the next three years, first in the Department of Employment and then in the Treasury, before I achieved permanent secretary rank in 1973.

For twenty years, from 1959 to 1979, the British establishment was mesmerised by the search for an instrument to control inflation through government intervention in the process by which working people's wages and salaries were determined. A huge amount of time and effort, as well as intellectual and nervous energy, was devoted by both Conservative and Labour governments to the attempt to find an effective incomes policy, which academic economists and Treasury officials were united in recommending as a kind of philosopher's stone to solve Britain's economic problems.

An astonishing variety of devices was tried out in this search: Harold Macmillan's Pay Pause of 1961; Aubrey Jones's Prices and Incomes Board of 1963; George Brown's Declaration of Intent of 1965; Ted Heath's statutory Pay Code of 1972; Jack Jones's Social Contract of 1975; and Denis Healey's budget of 1976 (which linked tax cuts to TUC agreement to a 3 per cent wage norm). Yet all of this was, in truth, to very little purpose. The impact of the various versions of incomes policy was analysed by my old DEA colleague Sam Brittan and his co-author Peter Lilley in their book *The Delusion of Incomes Policy*.[41] They dedicated it to Heath and Healey 'without whom this book would not have been possible' and it should perhaps be kept permanently in print as a warning to future generations.

This was the area on which I was required to concentrate under the newly elected Conservative government. Central to the work was the administration of the government's own decisions on the wages of the large number of people

41 Temple Smith, 1977

who were paid, directly or indirectly, out of the public purse – from civil servants to teachers, doctors, postmen, policemen, members of the armed forces and those employed in local authorities and nationalised industries. An interdepartmental committee of senior officials was set up to ensure consistency and conformity with the government's objectives by the relevant officials in these different areas. As the committee's chairman, I became the Great Panjandrum of incomes policy, so much so that when in 1975 I first met Margaret Thatcher, who had been Education Secretary in Heath's government but was now Leader of the Opposition, she characteristically greeted me with the words 'You are the man who wouldn't allow me to pay my teachers the salaries they deserved.'

With the full authority and support of Employment Secretary Robert Carr, a humane and thoughtful 'one nation' Tory with whom it was a pleasure to work, I used this committee to implement what became known as the 'n minus one' policy. This grew naturally out of our experience of public sector pay negotiations. It consisted of trying, within the limits of what was possible without provoking direct confrontation with the unions concerned, to lower the 'going rate' (or norm) of public sector pay settlements by small steps in successive wage negotiations. Thus, if the going rate of annual wage increases was, say, 12 per cent, we would aim to negotiate the next couple of settlements at around 10.5 per cent or 11 per cent and gradually bring the going rate down by a percentage point or more over a period of months. According to one of Heath's biographers[42] 'the informal n minus one policy of wage restraint worked remarkably well; by January 1972 the going rate of wage rises had fallen from an average of 14 per cent to nearer 9 per cent'. The 27 per cent settlement achieved by the miners, in the wake of their strike, in March 1972 was expected to kill off n minus one for good: but in fact this settlement proved to be a genuine exception and in the following three months thirty-three public sector settlements averaged only 9 per cent. In his speech to that year's party conference Heath said: 'We were given a mandate to reduce inflation. That meant bringing down inflationary wage settlements, as we have done. We have been given all too little credit for what we have done.'

Despite this, there was continued pressure on the government from academics, Treasury officials and outside commentators to introduce a statutory incomes policy. When further talks with the TUC ended without agreement, Heath yielded to this; in November he announced the imposition of a ninety-day freeze (renewable for a further thirty days, if required) covering all wages and salaries, rents and dividends and the prices of all goods and services except imports and fresh foods. I, for my sins, was given responsibility for preparing a detailed Pay Code to follow this – a piece of work which another of Heath's

42 John Campbell, *Edward Heath* (Jonathan Cape, 1993)

biographers described as 'an ingenious and labyrinthine mosaic of regulations'.[43]

I was also closely involved in the exhaustive internal discussions at No. 10 where the government's incomes policy was developed. But so far as policy formulation was concerned, the Prime Minister's principal adviser was William Armstrong, who appeared to revel in it with almost messianic zeal. In the field of incomes policy in particular, Armstrong's influence was immense, since the government decisions required were effectively taken by Heath personally and not by his Cabinet.

I had, of course, known Ted Heath at Oxford – not very well because the three-year age difference that there was between us is always more of a barrier then than it is in later life. I got to know him better in 1963, when he was Secretary of State for Regional Development and I was head of the division concerned in the Board of Trade. I have one abiding memory of him from those days, when I accompanied him on a visit to the mining areas in the North East, which were grappling with the fallout from widespread pit closures. At Heath's request we paid a visit to Durham Cathedral, where the Dean showed us round in the way that the rest of us do the honours in our own home. When we had absorbed

43 Philip Ziegler, *Edward Heath* (Harper Press, 2010)

the building's majestic beauty the Dean, Heath's private secretary and I sat down in the nave while Ted climbed into the organ loft. From there, for the next half hour, he treated us to a concert played on an organ built by the famous Durham firm that had supplied the instrument he played as organ scholar at Balliol. It was a delightful and memorable occasion which reminded us that, despite his awkward personality, there was a sensitive human being lurking somewhere inside the future Prime Minister.

Heath was a complex man – a loner who found it hard to make any kind of close personal relationship and famously had no small talk. In his address at Heath's memorial service in Westminster Abbey, Douglas Hurd told a story of how, as his political secretary at the time, he had accompanied Heath to a constituency dinner in Bexley. Hurd and the agent, who were sitting at the bottom of the table, noticed that Heath was hardly talking to his neighbour, a lady who was an influential supporter of the local party, so they sent a note up to him, advising him that the lady in question was important and that he should have a talk with her. Heath returned the note with the reply 'I have'. Doreen had a similar experience when sitting next to him at a private dinner given by the Seligmans. Searching around for something to talk about, she remembered that his yacht *Morning Cloud* had recently run aground on a sandbank near Ramsgate, which we had often sailed past in our own boat. When she commiserated with Ted about this, his reply was: 'The chart was wrong – I've written to the Hydrographer Royal to tell him so.'

Despite his often excruciating awkwardness in personal relationships, Heath was admired by many (including myself) when he became Prime Minister. Whether they agreed with his views or not, he came across to the general public as a straight-talking man of principle, who would fight for what he believed to be right and, with his modest background, would understand their concerns and needs. This contrasted with their perception of Harold Wilson as a rather devious man, defined by his own famous dictum that 'a week is a long time in politics', and it stood Heath in good stead in his protracted discussions with the TUC on incomes policy.

From the outset he had set himself the task of persuading the trade union leaders to join him in constructing an incomes policy which would enable the economy to grow fast enough to reduce unemployment without stoking the fires of wage inflation. The Permanent Secretary of the Department of Employment, Sir Denis Barnes, who had a wealth of experience in this field, advised him that 'the gap between the government and the unions could not be closed by any agreement which would be counter-inflationary'. Heath (and William Armstrong) refused to accept this. They were convinced that, if they were given an opportunity to explain the reality of the country's economic situation to the unions, reason would prevail.

In his attempt to achieve his objective, Heath invested a phenomenal amount of prime ministerial time and energy in the discussions and showed unlimited patience in his dealings with the TUC. By doing this he won the respect of virtually all the union leaders. Jack Jones[44] in particular, who was an intensely political man and not easy to please, developed a genuine admiration – and, I believe, almost affection – for the Prime Minister. But, as Barnes had predicted, it was not enough to lead to agreement between them and, despite the promise of its early days, Heath's premiership ended in failure. I saw the final stages of this process from close to, but by that time I was no longer working in Whitehall.

The statutory prices and incomes policy which followed the ninety-day pay and price freeze was a hugely complicated affair, with ramifications which ran right across Whitehall, and responsibility for its administration and the necessary central co-ordination was transferred to the Treasury before the freeze expired. I went with it and thus spent the last months of my civil service career in the department which I had put down as only my second choice back in 1947.

My transfer to the Treasury prompted an agreeable comment in the 'Men and Matters' column of the *Financial*

44 General Secretary, Transport and General Workers' Union 1969–78 and one of the most influential people in the Labour movement

Times[45] – a very rare event for a civil servant. After some pleasant references to my earlier career, to the love of sailing which I shared with Edward Heath and to my role in the 'n minus one' policy, it ended with the following:

> McIntosh's career has given him the kind of experience outside Whitehall which the Permanent Secretary of the Treasury, Sir Douglas Allen, has said he wants in the department. He also takes with him a reputation for openness and sociability. It remains to be seen whether he can withstand the Treasury's ability to remodel newcomers in its own image.

I think I can honestly say that I did.

It was in fact a congenial move for me because it meant that I would once again have Allen as my boss.[46] As had been the case in the DEA, we worked easily together, with Douglas rarely, if ever, interfering in my area of responsibility but always available to give me support or advice if I needed it. The nine months or so that I spent in Great George Street enabled me to get to know him better and deepened my respect and liking for him.

In the 1960s and '70s senior civil servants were still thought to belong to a rather elitist profession that drew its top people from the public schools and Oxbridge. It was

45 See Appendix IV

46 Allen had succeeded Roll as Permanent Secretary of the DEA in 1966 and moved to the Treasury when the DEA was abolished two years later

therefore noteworthy that Douglas was the son of a policeman and that the father of the man he succeeded as Head of the Civil Service in 1974 (William Armstrong) had been a Salvation Army bandsman. This was the kind of upward mobility for which my generation had voted in 1945, and it was good to see our hopes being realised in this way.[47]

Some months later Douglas told me that I was to be promoted to permanent secretary rank, as Director General of the National Economic Development Office. This was not strictly a civil service appointment; only three of the seven DGs who occupied the post in the thirty years of its existence were civil servants, the rest came from industry or (in one case) from academia. The DG's salary was paid from public funds but his appointment – or dismissal – required the agreement of all three bodies represented on the council, namely the government, the CBI and the TUC. So, while my new appointment carried with it permanent secretary rank and pay, I was not a member of the club of departmental heads in Whitehall who met monthly under the chairmanship of the Head of the Civil Service – and therefore not quite a mandarin. I was, however, delighted to be offered the job, for which my previous experience made me well prepared. I had by now had enough of Whitehall.

47 Yet according to a report by the Social Mobility Commission published in August 2014, only twenty-five out of 600 new recruits to the civil service fast-stream were from working class backgrounds in 2012. Sadly, we have gone backwards in this respect in the current century

As I made my move the curtain rose on a turbulent – and in retrospect almost surreal – period which has few parallels in British history.

–CHAPTER THIRTEEN–

NEDDY: PART 1

FROM ITS INCEPTION in 1962 the National Economic Development Council (NEDC) was universally known as Neddy. This was an engaging nickname for an official organisation – and indeed Neddy always seemed to be well regarded by the general public, probably because they saw it as a non-partisan body that was trying to do some good. The Council was made up of six Cabinet ministers, six representatives each from the CBI and the TUC, one from the City, a nationalised industry chairman, an independent member and the Director General. It met once a month, under the chairmanship of the Chancellor of the Exchequer or, from to time (usually about twice a year), the Prime Minister. Its work was supported by an office (NEDO) with a permanent staff of economists and other specialists, headed by the Director General and, with a few exceptions, recruited from outside Whitehall, and by a dozen or more 'Little Neddies', which were tripartite bodies concerned with individual industries.

Neddy was the joint brainchild of Harold Macmillan and his Chancellor of the Exchequer, Selwyn Lloyd. In his memoirs Macmillan gave the credit for coming up with the idea of Neddy to Lloyd, who seems to have seen it partly as a help in the attempt to get growth without inflation and partly as a means of introducing to this country something similar to the French system of indicative planning, which was highly thought of in Britain at the time. From all that I know and have read about Macmillan, with whom I had a talk about it some years later, I feel sure that in giving the idea his strong support he had two other considerations in mind as well. One was that as a new body, independent of Whitehall, NEDO might be more effective at identifying Britain's economic weaknesses and prescribing remedies for them than the Treasury, of which he had a poor opinion. The other was that the Neddy Council would provide a regular forum in which ministers and trade union leaders could exchange views on national problems and get to know one another personally, in a way which simply did not otherwise exist when the Conservatives were in power. I am sure it was this second point that particularly attracted Macmillan.

When I became involved with Neddy, indicative planning was already part of history, having been abandoned when the deflationary measures of 1966 and devaluation the following year torpedoed the Wilson government's National Plan. By the time Ted Heath became Prime Minister, the

Conservative Party had changed a good deal, with 'Selsdon Man'[48] foreshadowing the Thatcherism which was to come at the end of the decade. Macmillan's 'middle way' and 'one nation' attitudes towards the working class and trade unions (which stemmed from his experiences in the First World War and the depression of the 1930s) still had a good deal of support within the Tory Party: but they were balanced by a growing attachment to free market doctrine and opposition to the so-called 'corporatism' of bodies like the CBI and TUC (and hence, to some extent, of Neddy too). These divided attitudes within his party made life difficult for Heath in 1974 and contributed directly to his downfall.

As I took up my post in July 1973, the National Coal Board and the miners were approaching the start of their first wage negotiations since the whopping 27 per cent increase agreed after the previous year's strike. Not long afterwards, Ted Heath and William Armstrong had a private talk in the Downing Street garden with the miners' leader Joe Gormley from whom they thought they had received an assurance that the miners would settle within the limits of the government's statutory incomes policy. It soon turned out that either they had misunderstood what Gormley was telling them or he was promising an outcome which he couldn't deliver. It was perhaps a bit of both but

48 Before the 1970 election Heath held a brain-storming session of his shadow Cabinet at the Selsdon Park Hotel in Croydon. This came up with a radical free-market agenda which Harold Wilson described as the work of 'Selsdon Man'

nobody has been able – or will now be able – to establish what was actually said at their meeting, which was in any case overtaken by subsequent developments.

From October onwards, events unfolded with a remorseless inevitability which gave Robert Carr (by then Home Secretary) 'a sense of doom, as though a Greek tragedy was about to be acted out'. The trigger for this was the outbreak of war in the Middle East. This led OPEC to cut exports of oil by up to 25 per cent and to quadruple its price – measures which were bound to have a dire effect on both world trade and the domestic economy. By an unfortunate coincidence, OPEC's decision was followed within days by Heath's announcement of the terms of the statutory incomes policy which was to follow the wage freeze introduced earlier in the year. In framing the rules for Phase 3, as it was called, Heath had tried to leave room for a reasonable settlement for the miners – hence the importance of his talk with Gormley in the Downing Street garden – but he had also made plain his determination not to countenance any exceptions to the rules. In this way he had painted himself into a corner from which there was no escape when the Yom Kippur war moved the goalposts.

It is always hard for politicians to change carefully prepared plans when the context in which their decisions were taken changes. For Heath, who never took a decision until he was sure it was right, it was almost impossible. In the circumstances of winter 1973 (with the Sunningdale

Conference on Northern Ireland and a European Summit in Copenhagen taking place within days of one another) this was doubly true, as overwork and strain had brought him to a state of exhaustion. The reduced supply and increased price of oil gave hugely increased importance to uninterrupted coal production and transformed the miners' bargaining power. It was not difficult to see this; nor was anyone who knew the NUM[49] in any doubt that they would take advantage of it – as indeed many people would consider they were justified in doing. In the light of the new situation created by the Yom Kippur war, it would have been easy for Heath, if he had grasped the opportunity immediately, to make an exception for the miners without loss of face. I was particularly conscious of this because, while still in the Treasury, I was closely concerned with preparing the counter-inflation legislation introduced in 1972. I advised ministers at that time not to make the legislation so inflexible that, in the event of a serious industrial dispute, they could find themselves caught up in a situation from which there was no practical exit. This advice was not welcome: but I persevered and in the end it was accepted and a provision allowing ministers to override the terms of Phase 3 in exceptional circumstances was included in the legislation. However, this was never used.

Two days after Heath's announcement about Phase 3, the National Coal Board offered the miners the maximum

49 National Union of Mineworkers

increase permissible under its terms, which the NUM rejected. The Coal Board was widely criticised for going to the limit right away since it left the NUM no scope to employ its traditional tactic of making sure it secured some increase on the opening offer. In reality, I doubt whether the Coal Board had any choice; if they had offered less than the maximum permissible under Phase 3, the NUM team would almost certainly have walked out of the negotiations there and then. Towards the end of October Heath saw the NUM negotiators in Downing Street and did his best to persuade them to change their minds and accept the Coal Board's offer. He was not successful and when they reported back to their membership the next day the result was an overtime ban which came into force on 12 November. The government responded to this by declaring a national state of emergency. At this point the clock started ticking for a direct confrontation between the miners and the elected government which only the miners could win.

Although Neddy had hitherto avoided becoming involved in individual wage negotiations – which never benefit from being conducted on a public stage – it was closely concerned with the miners' dispute from now on. The gravity of the economic problems created by the seismic change in the oil market was soon widely recognised and it was plain that, with its weak balance of payments and troubled labour relations, Britain would find it particularly difficult to cope with the world recession everyone was predicting. It was clear to me that the next NEDC meeting, on 5 December, would provide an opportunity to try to develop a consensus round the Neddy table on how to tackle our new problems, which we should not allow to slip. In a busy forty-eight hours I took soundings from a number of influential Council members and found them all sympathetic to this idea.

The Neddy meeting, under the Chancellor Tony Barber's chairmanship, went well. The gravity of the situation – which one member described as the most dangerous we had faced since the 1930s – was generally recognised and there were constructive contributions from nearly everyone round the table. After a good, wide-ranging discussion, Barber, who had said little himself, asked me to sum up. I said we were all agreed that we faced a potentially very serious situation and it was clear we would not be able to deal with it if we remained divided by industrial conflict. While I didn't want to overrate what Neddy could do, if we didn't use it in a situation like this, we might as well wind it up. We had just had one of the most realistic discussions Neddy had had for years and we should resume it as soon as possible to consider what action was now required. Campbell Adamson, for the CBI, immediately suggested that we should meet again in emergency session before Christmas and Len Murray,[50] for the TUC, weighed in in support. Barber was doubtful but after some discussion it was agreed that we should meet on 21 December 'to take stock of a developing situation'.

50 General Secretary of the Trades Union Congress

Buoyed up by the progress we had made on the 5th, I spent the fortnight's interval before the next meeting listening and talking to a wide range of relevant people. From Douglas Allen I learned that the Treasury were very gloomy about the economic outlook and were forecasting a fall in Britain's GDP in 1974. Fredy Fisher, the editor of the *Financial Times*, agreed with this and also thought there was a real risk of a right wing, authoritarian government coming to power in the next twelve months. (This view was not uncommon at the time.) He added that, although Heath's attitude had clearly hardened, there was a body of opinion in the Cabinet (including Keith Joseph[51] and Margaret Thatcher) in favour of taking a conciliatory line with the miners. David Basnett, a member of what the TUC called their 'Neddy Six', was very critical of Heath and made it clear that, as others had told me, this view was now generally held in the TUC. He said that in 1972 Heath had been well regarded by the union leaders but about half way through the most recent set of talks his attitude had changed and he appeared to have written off the chances of reaching an agreement with them. Nevertheless, Basnett personally regarded the Neddy meeting on the 21st as very important and thought the Prime Minister should chair it.

Piers Dixon, a personal friend who was a Conservative backbencher and an officer of the 1922 Committee, told me that the Tory Party was unanimous in refusing to give way

51 Secretary of State for Social Services 1970–74

to the miners (a view which I discovered my friend Roy Jenkins shared) and was more united behind Heath than ever before. I found a quite different attitude in Scotland, when I flew there that week to deliver a speech at a CBI conference. I was struck by the gulf between the Scottish industrialists' views and what one heard in London; there was no talk up north of the need to 'stand firm and not give in to the unions' – they wanted to avoid damaging confrontation. Finally, the Governor of the Bank of England Gordon Richardson, Len Murray's predecessor Vic Feather and Campbell Adamson all told me that Ted Heath was suffering from acute fatigue which had seriously impaired his judgement.

On 13 December the Prime Minister announced that, in order to save electricity, a three-day working week for everyone except those engaged in essential services would come into force on 1 January. The next day we had a meeting of the 'Group of Four' to prepare the ground for the coming Council meeting. This group, which had been in existence for some years, consisted of the Permanent Secretary of the Treasury, the general secretary of the TUC and the directors general of the CBI and Neddy; it met about four times a year in the Neddy offices. The members of the group, who were not allowed to send substitutes to the meetings, exchanged views with complete freedom, in the certain knowledge that they would not be reported to anyone else, and no record was circulated. After this meeting Douglas

Allen told me that a number of ministers (which I guessed included Barber) had now written off the TUC because it could never deliver anything.

Two days before the special Neddy meeting I lunched with Sidney Greene, the senior member of the TUC's Neddy Six, a wise and experienced man whom I liked and respected. He told me that the TUC General Council had had a good meeting that morning. Everything he said bore out my belief that the unions were not looking for a new confrontation with the government; he fully realised that Heath would need help to climb down from the exposed position to which he had committed himself and said the unions would do their best to build a ladder for him, if required. I then had another talk with Douglas Allen, whose final words to me were that nothing on earth would induce Heath to give the miners anything over and above Phase 3. Returning to my office I found my predecessor Frank Figgures, now chairman of the Pay Board, waiting in my office. He said it was quite clear that the miners would not settle within Phase 3: the only question therefore was whether the government should amend the rules to accommodate them or use the escape clause in the Counter-Inflation Act which allowed them to override the rules in exceptional circumstances. When Frank had left I went with Len Murray to a well-attended party at the National Institute for Economic and Social Research, where everyone I spoke to wished me luck at the Neddy meeting. They all wanted it to succeed.

Armed with the information and opinions I had garnered, I went the following day to the NEDC meeting, which the Prime Minister chaired. It was a disaster.

The meeting began with a brief introduction by Heath, who referred to the fact that the country was facing a number of different problems, due partly to industrial action and partly to the situation in the Middle East. He then gave me a half-hearted invitation to introduce the paper I had circulated which he clearly expected me to decline. I decided not to be put off by this and spoke for about five minutes, in which I stressed the need to get down urgently to an analysis of the changes which the oil crisis would give rise to here, so that we could maximise the advantages we had through our coal and North Sea oil reserves. As far as I could tell this went down quite well and even Heath grunted approvingly.

We then had a couple of hours' discussion of the three-day week, which was due to come into effect in ten days. For a long time this consisted of a reasoned dialogue between the representatives of the TUC who, because of its effect on their members' pay packets, were desperate to get the three-day week dropped or postponed, and the CBI. For the second time in a month I felt that the NEDC was doing the job for which it was created. Then Heath joined in, saying that the three-day week was all the miners' fault and that the government had a responsibility to see that industry didn't grind to a halt, as happened in 1972. Unfortunately, he spoke for too long and too forcefully, dominating the meeting in a way which might just have been acceptable in Cabinet but was quite inappropriate in a tripartite body. This lack of sensitivity to his surroundings showed him at his worst.

As we broke for lunch we learned that the Coal Board and the NUM, who had also been meeting that morning, had agreed to make a joint approach to the Pay Board on some point relating to their wage negotiations. After lunch I had a short private talk with Heath. I told him that I had spoken to all the trade union members of Neddy recently and that they were more willing than I had ever known them to reach an agreement with the government. I added that I thought that, if he showed his old patience, he could get a worthwhile statement from the TUC which could be used after the Neddy meeting. Heath asked me some questions about this and I then left, as we were joined by Barber and Whitelaw,[52] with whom Heath remained closeted for the next half hour.

The afternoon session was very depressing. We had a desultory discussion of the long term for an hour or so, with myself and others trying hard to keep it going despite the obvious lack of interest of ministers and the trade union people, who simply wanted to know how the miners' negotiations were progressing. After a while

52 Whitelaw was by then Secretary of State for Employment, having just been brought back from Northern Ireland to take up this post

discussion returned to the three-day week. Sidney Greene argued strongly for a postponement, if only until after the next meeting between the Coal Board and the NUM. But Heath was resolutely opposed to this and so were the CBI. It was clear that the Prime Minister had put the shutters up.

There followed a short adjournment to meet the TUC's request for more information about the coal negotiations and as I recorded in my diary at the time:

> From then on the Prime Minister was tense and irritable. During the adjournment everyone hung around feeling miserable and trying to think of some way to avert the breakdown ... I felt unutterably depressed. It is a dreadful thing to sit and watch a country slide into chaos, through the obstinacy of a few individuals, and be powerless to stop it even in a central position like mine.
>
> I cannot believe that the miners will settle next Thursday and I am sure that the three-day week will cause great bitterness and will mean that we face the tremendous problems which the oil crisis will bring, as a divided country. I have been forced today to revise my opinion of Heath, whom I have hitherto greatly admired, despite his obvious weaknesses. I now think that he is behaving irresponsibly – the miners will get a settlement outside Phase 3 in the end; and even if they don't, the damage done by the three-day week will outweigh the temporary victory over the militants. Heath thinks he is fighting for a great principle – but the fact is he can't

see the wood (i.e. the enormous national problem created by the oil crisis) for the trees (i.e. Mick McGahey[53] and co. in the NUM).

During the Christmas break that followed the Neddy meeting, OPEC announced a further sharp increase in the price of oil. On 1 January the three-day week came into operation; we all held meetings by candlelight and a deep sense of crisis ensued. The gap between those who thought it imperative to stand firm against the miners and those who wanted to find a way out of the impasse widened. Opinion on both sides hardened and the emotional temperature rose. The next monthly meeting of Neddy was due on the 9th and I thought that, after the depressing outcome of the last meeting, it was important to hold this one as planned – one of Neddy's advantages had always been that the three parties attended the regular council meetings as a matter of course, however bad their relations in public might be at the time. Len Murray and Campbell Adamson both agreed with this as, after some discussion, did Tony Barber, when I went to see him and Douglas Allen on 2 January. Douglas told me later that ministers were unhappy about holding the Neddy meeting but he thought he had persuaded them to do so. As I recorded at the time: 'He then said, in a menacing tone, that if the TUC used the meeting for political purposes it would be the last NEDC meeting to be held.'

53 McGahey was the Communist vice-president of the NUM who had told the Prime Minister at an earlier Downing Street meeting that his objective was to bring about a change of government

After this talk with Allen I spoke to Adamson who said that in no circumstances would the CBI encourage a breach of Phase 3 at this stage. On the day before the meeting I told Murray that somebody would have to introduce some mobility into the situation – otherwise the three parties would go on glowering at one another from their trenches until the country ground to a halt. It seemed clear that neither the government nor the CBI would move, so the TUC would have to. Murray listened carefully and said he didn't know how the next day's TUC meeting would go – but couldn't the CBI join the TUC in asking for the miners to be made an exception?

And so we reached the Neddy meeting of 9 January – a day which is permanently etched in my memory. As this was an episode of some historical significance, I quote my contemporary record of the meeting in full:

Wednesday 9 January 1974

I spent all morning preparing my notes for introducing our paper at the council meeting. The great thing is to get the ending right so that if the TUC or CBI are ready to make a move they can pick up naturally something I have referred to in my opening remarks.

I went home for lunch and in the middle of it, Len Murray rang. He told me – strictly for my own information – that the TUC would be making a statement at the Neddy meeting to the effect that if the miners were given an increase outside Phase 3, other unions would not pray it in aid in their negotiations. I said this sounded excellent. Len said it wasn't exactly excellent but it might provide a piece of cotton for people to pull and that, if they did, it might turn out to have a three-inch rope on the end of it. He said it would be particularly helpful if the CBI could say something which would enable the TUC to make their statement naturally. Len added that the decision to make it was unanimous and that Jones and Scanlon[54] were completely committed to it.

I tracked down Campbell Adamson at the London Chamber of Commerce and left a message asking him to look in on me before the council meeting. When he did so I told him that Len had been in touch with me since his TUC meeting and that it looked as though there might be some possibility of movement by the TUC. I didn't tell him what form it would take but suggested it might help if he were to say something, before the TUC came in, about the CBI's worries that high settlements in one industry could lead to a burst of inflationary settlements in other industries. In passing, Campbell congratulated me on the close relationship which I had built up with Len Murray. He thought this was very helpful.

I thought seriously about whether I should phone Douglas Allen to let him know of the new development but came to the conclusion it was too big a risk to take. I suspect that the government are

54 President, Amalgamated Union of Engineering Workers

so dug in that they would try to stifle any TUC initiative at birth if they heard of it in advance. When Douglas spoke to me yesterday on the telephone he said that if the TUC used today's meeting for political purposes it would be Neddy's last meeting. I do not believe this for a moment – the government is in no position to do without Neddy in this time of national crisis and strife. But the conversation worried me because it seemed to indicate that Douglas had become infected with the neurotic attitude which Barber and others are now showing towards the TUC.

When the Council began I gave a longish introduction to our paper on the effect of the three-day week. The gist of it was that if three-day working lasted only until the end of January the consequences would be manageable and recovery reasonably quick; but that if it continued into February we should run into problems of an altogether different order and the effect on output, exports and eventual recovery would get quickly and cumulatively worse.

Len Murray and Campbell Adamson both agreed with our analysis. Campbell broadened the discussion out a bit with a reference to the miners and Phase 3. Sidney Greene then came in with the TUC statement which Len Murray had told me about. He said that if the government made a settlement with the miners possible (i.e. outside Phase 3) the TUC and the trade union movement would not use this in other negotiations or quote it as an excuse for other exceptional settlements. He said that they were willing to make this offer in order to get the miners' settlement out of the way and so bring three-day working to an end. After a pause in which most of us held our breath, Barber said, 'Does this mean that the TUC is ready to agree to a tripartite incomes policy with statutory back-up powers for groups which don't conform?' I could hardly believe my ears when I heard this tendentious question and the hostile tone in which it was asked. But Sidney, imperturbable as ever, simply repeated the TUC assurance.

There followed a lively discussion in which all the TUC team spoke up in favour of their offer. In the course of it Sidney said two things which seemed significant to me. One was that the TUC were 'against inflation and wanted to control it'; the other was that unions would 'instruct their negotiators to abide by the TUC assurance'. Barber intervened three or four times – each time in a negative and hostile tone. He said several times that HMG would not in any circumstances contemplate any settlement outside Phase 3. The CBI team mostly sat silent – except for Dick Marsh,[55] who tried to probe the TUC offer to see what it really meant, their interventions were unconstructive.

I imagine that most people round the table were as startled as I was at the Chancellor's brusque rejection of the offer. One would have expected him to be more adroit, however much he disliked it. Sidney Greene pressed him to consider it seriously. Barber said he would report it to Willie Whitelaw, to which Greene said, 'That's not good enough: you should report it to yourself and to Ted because I reckon if you two don't agree then it won't be agreed and if you do it will.' Barber simply repeated that it would be wrong to think that the government would be prepared

55 Richard Marsh (1928–2011), a former Labour Cabinet minister, was chairman of British Rail

to settle any individual case outside Phase 3. Hugh Scanlon said that in that case the TUC might well decide to withdraw their offer.

At this stage I came to the conclusion that if someone didn't try to rescue it the TUC offer might founder. So I intervened as follows. I said the DG of Neddy was the last person to want to get involved in an individual dispute. However, the afternoon's discussion had flowed from a statement by myself about the three-day week which showed how serious the consequences for the economy would be if it were prolonged. We must also bear in mind that the brunt would be borne not by people like ourselves but by weekly paid manual workers. The TUC had made a statement that seemed to me to be very important – like all such statements it was no doubt imperfect but it might provide a basis on which people could build. It was important to record accurately what the TUC had said and, subject to correction, I would record that:

- The TUC team had given an assurance (in the terms used by Sidney) on behalf of the General Council and the trade union movement and had said that negotiators would be instructed to abide by it;

- The TUC had recognised the need to control inflation;

- They had made no request that the government should repeal the Counter-Inflation Act or amend the Pay Code.

Silence followed and after a short discussion about what should be said to the press we adjourned.

My personal involvement in the discussions on the TUC offer came to an end at this point. Over the next ten days the Prime Minister had two discussions with the TUC in Downing Street, the first of which lasted for an almost unbelievable five and a half hours. Murray told me afterwards that it had been a puzzling occasion in which Whitelaw had been actively exploring the possibility of a deal, the Prime Minister had shown some interest in one and Barber, while not questioning the TUC's good faith, had taken a thoroughly negative line. Both meetings concentrated on the TUC's capacity to deliver and the level at which the miners might agree to settle. Heath and his colleagues pressed the TUC to say whether, if the miners were given a settlement outside Phase 3, they could guarantee that other unions would not claim exceptional treatment too. The TUC were, of course, unable to give any such guarantee; their constitutional relationship with their member unions was not of that kind. The General Council of the TUC had great authority within the trade union movement but there was no way they could compel individual unions to follow the policies they laid down, any more than the CBI could force individual member companies to follow theirs. However, in making their offer at the Neddy meeting the TUC had gone a long way in this direction, notably by saying that they would instruct union negotiators to abide by the terms laid down in the offer – wording which was without precedent in TUC documents.

It was also clear that in the economic climate created by the oil crisis and the three-day week the overwhelming majority of unions would have to settle within the terms of Phase 3 anyway; even Hugh Scanlon said publicly that his union, the AEUW, would not press its claim beyond the limits of Phase 3. The only clear exceptions to this were the electricians, whose leadership was virulently anti-Communist and would not want to make life unduly difficult for the government at this particular moment, and the tanker drivers, who could perhaps be considered as entitled to special treatment because of the oil crisis. If therefore the government were to accept the TUC offer and to frame its actions accordingly it would have to be prepared to take a certain amount on trust from the TUC. Margaret Thatcher understood this – in a television interview in 1977, when she was the leader of her party, she said with reference to the 1974 dispute: 'One thing which Len Murray said which we have not given him enough credit for was when he offered to accept that the miners could be made a special case – this was a very responsible proposal and I am sorry that we did not follow it up.' But in 1974 Thatcher's voice did not count for very much in Cabinet compared with heavyweights such as Peter Carrington, Jim Prior, Tony Barber and Peter Walker.[56] They were all hard-liners who refused to contemplate any settlement outside Phase 3 and – especially in the case of the first two, who were respectively chairman and vice-chairman of the party – reflected the more or less unanimous view of Tory backbenchers that the government must not 'give in to the miners'. Willie Whitelaw, on the other hand, told me in October 1974 that he was never in any doubt that the miners' claim should have been settled at the best level obtainable before Christmas 1973 in the wake of the oil crisis and that he regretted not having pushed this point of view harder. This was, of course, exactly my own view.

Heath himself seemed ambivalent. As an intelligent and well-intentioned man, all his instincts inclined him to avoid a direct confrontation with the unions. But by nailing his colours to the mast of 'no exceptions to Phase 3' he had made this impossible; and, like John Major twenty years later and David Cameron in 2013, he was boxed in by the hard men behind him. My feeling was that, having (as by then I think he recognised) missed his opportunity to solve the miners' dispute at the time of the original OPEC decision, he was simply bewildered and at a loss to know what to do next. His own as yet undiagnosed thyroid condition and the fact that his principal adviser was having apocalyptic visions and was on the verge of a mental collapse

56 Secretary of State for Trade and Industry

cannot have helped. He deserved better advice from those around him than he received. On 21 January – less than two weeks after the Neddy meeting – I recorded that 'the TUC offer now seems to be dead'. Three days later the NUM decided to ballot their members on strike action which, unsurprisingly, was approved. From then on an election was inevitable.

For my own part I am sorry, with hindsight, that I did not give Douglas Allen some advance warning about the TUC's offer. I was not at liberty to be specific but I could have passed on to him what Len Murray had said to me about a cotton thread which might have a three-inch rope attached to it and trusted him to make use of this if he thought it would be helpful. The reason I didn't pass it on was that I thought my old friend had been infected with the prevailing neurosis: but perhaps I had been infected too. It was a time of great tension – inevitably so, because the stakes were so high. However, I do not believe that if I had given the government advance warning of the TUC's offer it would have altered the final outcome.

–CHAPTER FOURTEEN–

NEDDY: PART 2

THE ELECTORATE PRODUCED a hung Parliament, with neither of the main parties securing an overall majority. When Ted Heath's attempt to form a coalition with the Liberals failed, Harold Wilson became Prime Minister, with Denis Healey at the Exchequer.

Wilson, like Heath, was suffering from an as yet undiagnosed illness, which led to his resignation two years later. His energy had manifestly diminished since the days when I attended his Cabinet meetings in the 1960s and, as time went on, I detected a sharp lowering of his threshold of boredom in dealing with the multitude of issues which cross a Prime Minister's desk. But his current objective was a simple one: to make sure that the next election, which everyone expected to come before the end of the year, gave him a working majority. This was the sort of thing he was good at and rather enjoyed.

The national mood was sombre. Everybody knew that, following the oil crisis and the miners' strike, the economy was in very poor shape and the hung Parliament suggested that the voters had little confidence in the politicians' ability to put things right. This gave a boost to Neddy, which was seen as a non-partisan body that stood for the co-operation the country needed rather than the confrontation which led to the three-day week. Wilson, who had always been keen on Neddy, encouraged this; an unprecedented seven ministers attended the first Council meeting after the election. Perhaps more surprisingly, after Heath and Barber's ambivalence towards it, support for Neddy grew on the Conservative side. Their manifesto for the second general election of 1974 declared their intention to strengthen Neddy; I was told that they had nothing radical in mind but would rather build on a body which existed and worked well than create something new. Support for Neddy was strong in the CBI, whose president Harold Watkinson had been a member of Macmillan's Cabinet when the NEDC was formed and shared his belief in the 'middle way'. However, the arrival of a Labour government altered the dynamics of council meetings as the trade union leaders were already in direct contact with ministers on most of the issues under discussion. Jack Jones, in particular, saw no need to share his innermost thoughts in a tripartite forum when he could do it more effectively over a brandy in No. 10.

During the eight months' interval between the two elections public concern over the economy and the large number of inflationary wage settlements (including, of course, the post-election settlement with the miners, which even they may have considered generous) steadily deepened. By November 1974 – a month after the second election – there was a palpable feeling of crisis in the air. In private conversations I heard a lot of talk about an impending collapse and many normally sensible people predicted that some kind of authoritarian government would emerge before a year was out. As well as industrialists and bankers – and the Communist general secretary of the film workers – these included senior civil servants, among them the Permanent Secretary of the Treasury, Douglas Wass. Chatting with Arthur Peterson, my old boss at the DEA who was by then Permanent Secretary of the Home Office, I mentioned that the Treasury seemed reluctant to show any of their cards to Neddy. Peterson's reply was that this was because they didn't have any – no one in Whitehall had any idea how to handle the present crisis. Even Healey admitted to me privately that there was clearly a possibility that we should have a crash by Easter but added that there was still a chance that wages could be held to reasonable levels and a collapse avoided.

I thought that Neddy was in a good and, because of its membership, perhaps unique position to help out at this time of national crisis. I did everything I could to make sure that Council meetings were constructive and that I could truthfully report to the media afterwards that the government, the employers and the trade unions were doing their best to tackle the country's problems in a spirit of co-operation rather than conflict. This was potentially important for business confidence, which Campbell Adamson and others were telling us was so low that most companies were postponing any investment projects they could.

I spent a great deal of time and energy making our activities better known; for example, on the many visits I paid to factories, oil rigs, construction sites and so on I always asked if I could meet the local shop stewards, who were thought at that time to possess more power than their union leaders. To begin with, the managers were sceptical about this and thought it a waste of time: but the talks I had with the shop stewards invariably went well and, whatever they reported to their members afterwards, they listened to what I had to say in a friendly and not unhelpful way. I also spent time, at their request, with groups who were not represented on the NEDC – including retailers, architects, chambers of commerce, consumer associations and the Greater London Council. To someone in my non-partisan position it seemed that, in a very British way, almost everyone wanted to help to get the country out of the mess it was in and if that was what Neddy was trying to do they would like to be part of it.

The doctrine I was trying to propagate was that the problems Britain faced were deep-seated and could not be solved by any short-term fix: what was needed was a programme of action which would take more than the lifetime of a single parliament to complete. This approach, though no more than plain common sense, took me into political territory. I wanted in particular, to try to combat the growing perception of Neddy by some members of the Conservative Party as 'corporatist'. This perception was quite strongly held by many of their younger MPs, who thought that Macmillan's 'middle way' philosophy was paternalist and that bodies like the CBI and Neddy were undemocratic. Leaving aside the merits or demerits of this view, I argued that the country was in deep crisis and that, if Neddy could help, it should be encouraged to do so, corporatist or not.

Following this line of thought, I invited Keith Joseph, the leading thinker on the right of the Tory Party, to lunch. He started off brisk and suspicious – it was clear that he didn't have much use for Neddy and thought the lunch would probably be a waste of time. But as the meal went on he relaxed and, though I don't think we would ever have become soul mates, we had a very good talk. He sent me a nice letter afterwards thanking me for 'a very civilised and worthwhile lunch'.

I also accepted most of the many invitations I received to make speeches or give lectures at conferences, trade association dinners and the like. These gave me a platform to develop the theme of the need for a considered, and so far as possible bipartisan, industrial strategy to arrest the economic decline in which the country appeared to be trapped. I took great trouble over these speeches, which seemed to strike a strong chord with most of my listeners and, as they were usually well reported in the press and by the BBC, gave me quite a high profile nationally. I also gave a press conference after each monthly meeting of the NEDC and, given the troubled times we were living in, these were always well attended. I was very fortunate in that the journalists who covered Neddy at the time were an unusually talented lot. They included three men with whom I have enjoyed lasting friendships: Peter Hennessy and Andrew Adonis, who then worked for *The Times* and the *Financial Times* respectively and are now both members of the House of Lords, and William Keegan who, forty years on, still writes an influential column in *The Observer*. The late Dominick Harrod, whose father had been a leading Oxford economist when I was an undergraduate, reported on our work assiduously for the BBC and used to record an interview with me after almost every Council meeting.

I did not seek to provoke political controversy, but I was conscious that I was walking on thin ice and was not altogether surprised when Denis Healey told a journalist that 'the trouble with Ronnie McIntosh is that he thinks he is Jesus Christ – only Ronnie McIntosh and the NEDC can save Britain' and this appeared (without attribution) in the next issue of the *Investors Chronicle*. However, I was pleased that it was balanced by a leader in *The Guardian* about the same time which said: 'Neddy has survived the comings and goings of administrations and has built up a valuable stock of authority and expertise; indeed its reputation probably stands as high now as it has ever done.'

Life was not, however, all doom and gloom. In March 1975 I went with Doreen and my eldest niece Elizabeth to Buckingham Palace for my investiture as a KCB. There were four knights to be dubbed that year. I went first, followed by Maurice Oldfield, who was 'C' of the Secret Intelligence Service at the time, and Alan Walker, the chairman of a major brewing company. Then a separate door opened and in came a small figure in a wheelchair who made his way towards the Queen with tears running down his face. This was Charlie Chaplin, a boyhood hero of mine and perhaps the most popular film star of his day. While living in California he had in recent years been through a rough and unpleasant time because of a widely held belief in the United States that he was a Communist and possibly a Soviet agent. This had taken its toll on him and he could not contain his joy at being accorded such splendid recognition in the country of his birth.

Continuing the Communist theme, a month later I flew to Aberdeen for the annual conference of the Scottish TUC, which was completely controlled by the Communists. After dinner I went to a reception given by the *Morning Star* where I was told all the principal delegates would be. I saw the paper's industrial correspondent Mick Costello, whom I knew, and went up to him for a chat. He introduced me to Ted Heath's old bugbear Mick McGahey, who was standing next to him, and at that moment the band struck up the Internationale. So I found myself in a public place, singing what words of the red anthem I could remember in company with the two best-known Communists in Britain. I was lucky that there were no photographers nearby.

A few weeks after this Doreen and I gave an evening party for Sidney Greene and his wife. Sid had been a founding member of the NEDC, on which he had served without a break until 1975, and was about to retire. The Council's first chairman, Selwyn Lloyd, made a delightful speech in which he referred to the setting up of Neddy and how much he had enjoyed chairing it 'until for reasons which even now I do not wholly understand I was removed from the scene'. Harold Wilson followed and said that Neddy had never been stronger than it was now, and then Sidney made a nice little speech in which he referred to 'our friend Ted' who was also there. It was altogether a very good occasion that showed the British establishment at its most civilised.

The expertise which *The Guardian* referred to as a characteristic of Neddy came from the specialist staff employed by NEDO and the external advisers on whom it could call, and from the Little Neddies, whose activities ensured that the staff's views were firmly rooted in reality. NEDO was made up of four divisions, all of which were headed at that time by experienced, well-motivated men of high calibre. The Economic Director, David Stout, was a New Zealand-born

Fellow of University College, Oxford who did some valuable original work during his time at Neddy comparing industrial productivity in Britain, Europe and the USA. The Industrial Director Bernard Asher was a positive thinker, on secondment from the American telecommunications company ITT, who went on to have a distinguished career in the City. The Manpower division was run by two experienced former trade union officials, Cyril Leach from the TUC and later John Cousins, who had been a national officer in Jack Jones's Transport and General Workers' Union. The fourth division, the Secretariat, was headed by Chris Lucas, a Treasury under-secretary of independent mind who, despite his provenance, was wholly committed to Neddy. It was a strong team whose work won the respect of all the Council members, including successive Chancellors (though not always of their officials, who tended to resent NEDO's incursions on to what they regarded as their exclusive turf).

This was the team that prepared the material on which our papers to the Council – and many of my speeches about the need for a bipartisan strategy to reverse our industrial decline – were based. David Stout's analytical work focused in particular on Britain's poor record on productivity, its persistent shortages of skilled labour and the widespread under-utilisation of industrial capacity, reflecting a failure to make products of the quality, design and reliability that potential customers were looking for. (It is depressing to note that these same weaknesses are still with us and holding back national growth forty years later.)

As the months progressed and the national economy deteriorated, the idea of developing an agreed plan to get to grips with these weaknesses gradually gained ground. Harold Wilson was attracted by the idea and as support grew in the press, the CBI and elsewhere, he decided to chair a special all-day meeting of NEDC at Chequers to launch what came to be called the new industrial strategy. This was to consist of two parts. The first was to be an agreement by all three bodies on NEDC that the country should give higher priority to manufacturing industry; that, in taking decisions on matters such as taxation, public procurement, regional policy and labour legislation the government should give priority to industry's needs; and that the continuity of policy required for this should be maintained over a period of years. The second part, which was to be based on the Little Neddies and organised by NEDO, was to involve the adoption of a tripartite approach to improvements in industrial performance in some forty sectors of industry, which between them covered over two thirds of manufacturing and exports. This was similar to the work done by a series of Anglo-American 'productivity committees' set up under the Marshall Plan, whose work in the immediate aftermath of World War Two was generally respected.

The Chequers meeting, though in some respects a typical Wilson public relations exercise, went well. The Prime

Minister himself was in sparkling form and spoke effectively both at the meeting and at the subsequent press conference. Healey also spoke well and gave the 'new industrial strategy' his warm support; and the day's discussion was, on the whole, realistic and constructive. Press reaction the following day was sceptical but the *Financial Times* had a warily favourable leader and most of the other papers regarded the outcome as mildly encouraging. I began to think, with my usual unquenchable optimism, that we might be about to achieve a breakthrough in tackling our deep-seated problems.

Unfortunately, within a few weeks the government dealt the new strategy a body blow by its handling of the Chrysler crisis. Chrysler's UK operation, which employed around 17,000 people, was plagued by unofficial labour stoppages and losing money. Its American parent company proposed to close it unless the government agreed to finance a rescue operation. The Industry Minister, Eric Varley, wanted to take a tough line and save public funds for more worthwhile projects and threatened to resign if he didn't get his way. But Wilson over-ruled him and the government gave the company nearly £200 million without any strings. Political opinion on the pros and cons of subsidising a 'lame duck' to maintain employment was deeply divided. I was on Varley's side and recorded in my diary that 'the general feeling is that this will mean the death knell of the Chequers strategy'. A month is a long time in politics.

In early March 1976 Wilson chaired his last Neddy meeting and shortly afterwards resigned as Prime Minister on health grounds. By the time his successor Jim Callaghan took over, the outlook for the economy had taken a dramatic turn for the worse. There was no single trigger for this. It was rather a question of a growing recognition that the underlying problems of inflation, low productivity and excessive public borrowing, which had been ignored during the previous year's drift, were growing steadily worse and that there was no solution for them in sight. There was a widespread perception – especially overseas – that Britain was in a state of terminal decline, which it had neither the will nor the ability to reverse. The effect on sterling was predictable: at the beginning of April the pound fell sharply and the decline continued without let up until the IMF arrived six months later. There was much talk of national collapse and there were plenty of people who believed that we would not put our house in order until this happened.

Jim Callaghan made a good start as Prime Minister, performing well in Parliament, handling the trade unions skilfully and emphasising the need for everyone to pull together to get the country out of its economic difficulties. He reminded me very much of Stanley Baldwin, who had been Prime Minister in my schooldays. Very early on in his premiership he decided to chair a meeting of NEDC, which he did very effectively. He was – and remained – a strong supporter of the industrial strategy agreed at Chequers and breathed new life into it at this meeting. In addition, he made a point of inviting the CBI president Harold Watkinson, who had taken a very constructive line at the meeting, and Alf Allen, who was now the leader of the TUC's Neddy Six, to sit beside him at the subsequent press conference. This gave the meeting a national, non-party flavour. The next day Eric Varley made a statement in Parliament about the meeting, which was something I had been urging on the Prime Minister as a way of dealing with the criticism that Neddy was corporatist and undemocratic.

From the start, Callaghan and Healey made great efforts to reach a counter-inflationary agreement with the TUC over wages. In his April 1976 budget Healey introduced a complex provision making certain tax cuts conditional on TUC agreement to abide by a 3 per cent norm for wages. The TUC didn't like being put on the spot in this way but eventually reached agreement on the basis of a 4.5 per cent norm. I thought that this had a reasonable chance of holding but that unless it was complemented by cuts in public expenditure, it would not restore confidence in sterling, which continued its relentless decline.

A week later I recorded in my diary that:

> Reflecting on the Budget and the economic situation generally, I have a sense of doom today. For the first time I feel that the financial

> collapse, which so many people have said was imminent at various times in the last two years, may really be on its way. The fall in the value of sterling which has taken place in the last few weeks is very dramatic and shows that foreigners don't believe we are capable of managing our affairs effectively.

Events in the following months bore out my forebodings. The pound continued to fall and it became clear to me that the market's principal concern was now not so much inflationary wage settlements as the size of the public sector deficit. In a conversation I had with him at a CBI dinner I made this point to the Prime Minister, who did not disagree but said 'the trouble is where do you make the cuts?' which I didn't find reassuring. In July Denis Healey announced a package of economic measures. These included a reduction of £2 billion in the borrowing requirement but only half of this was to come from cuts in public expenditure; the rest would be achieved by an increase in employers' national insurance contributions and would add to industry's costs.

At the end of September the Labour Party conference voted against any cuts in public expenditure and, as I had expected, the pound plummeted. Callaghan made an orthodox right-wing speech, with all the right noises, but the pound continued to fall and it was evident that the market no longer had any confidence in the government's ability to deal with the nation's problems. While the Prime Minister was at the conference, the Chancellor and the Governor of the Bank of England were on their way to Heathrow to fly to Manila for the annual meeting of the IMF: but in a dramatic move – and as some said, after heavy pressure from the Governor – they turned back. Denis Healey flew instead to Blackpool where he announced that the government was applying to the IMF for a conditional loan – that is, the kind of bail-out with which we have become familiar through the troubles of Greece and other countries in the eurozone crisis of 2009–12.

Three weeks later, when I was in Switzerland for a conference, the Consul-General arranged for me to meet some 'gnomes of Zurich' (as Swiss foreign exchange dealers were often called in those days) over lunch. They turned out to be highly intelligent, friendly bankers who were well informed about Britain and regular visitors to London. We talked throughout the lunch about Britain's difficulties, which, as I expected, they attributed above all to excessive levels of public expenditure on non-productive activities.

In the weeks before negotiations with the IMF began in November the crisis deepened. Ted Heath, by now a bruised and resentful backbencher, made a powerful speech underlying its gravity; Harold Macmillan emerged from retirement to call for a government of national unity to prevent irreversible national decline; and the Prime Minister spoke publicly of the possibility of dictatorship if we couldn't solve the crisis.

At the beginning of December I added my voice to the debate. First, I delivered a lecture[57] at Reading University about the new industrial strategy, which Healey and Callaghan considered 'a very good statement of our industrial policy' and circulated to Cabinet.[58] Then I made a speech to a distinguished gathering of about 200 Fellows (now called Companions) of the British Institute of Management, including a large number of company chairmen and permanent secretaries. I was aware that in doing so I was bound to encroach on the politicians' territory, but I was quite clear in my own mind that, holding the position I did, it was right at a time of acute national crisis for me to make my views known and that, if my fellow-members of NEDC didn't like what I said, they were free to find another Director General.

I took great trouble over the BIM speech. Its general message was that we should switch resources out of non-productive activities – which I called the soft underbelly of the economy – into the productive sectors and give priority to 'the sharp end', that is, to industry. This would entail cuts in non-productive public expenditure but their deflationary effect should be offset by various expansionary measures, which might include a modest reduction in direct taxation.

---

57 *Future British Industrial Srategy: The 1976 Merchantile Credit Lecture,* published by Reading University

58 Healey to Callaghan, November 1976, National archives PREM 16/825

My speech was very fully reported in the media, with favourable leaders in the *Financial Times*, which emphasised that both the CBI and the TUC ought to be able to support my general thesis, and in the *Sunday Times*. It provoked an immediate, critical statement from the TUC, followed by an apologetic call from Len Murray, who said that if they had read the full text before their meeting they might well have reacted differently because there was a lot in it they would have liked. In response to a Parliamentary Question about it the Prime Minister said that 'the speech was rather like the curate's egg – it was good in parts; there were some parts I found myself in agreement with more than others'. It also brought me an attempted dressing down by Denis Healey[59] and an invitation from Buckingham Palace to have luncheon with the Queen.

As I recorded at the time:

Wednesday 15 December 1976

I went today to a small lunch at Buckingham Palace. It was an informal and delightful occasion – though unfortunately one to which spouses were not invited. Prince Philip went out of his way to let me know that he thought well of my recent speeches. I said I had been greatly cheered to find him saying very similar things in his own speeches to which he replied that he, like me, had been surprised at the publicity given to speeches which were doing no more than saying the obvious.

59 See *Challenge to Democracy*, diary entry for 10 December 1976

> I sat on the Queen's right at lunch. She talked to me for the first half of the meal – interestingly, informally and with great charm and naturalness. She had evidently discussed my BIM speech with Callaghan, who had told her that it 'stated the priorities very clearly'.[60] I was immensely cheered by her attitude and Prince Philip's towards it. The Queen has a nice wry sense of humour.

I remembered this when, at the time of her Diamond Jubilee in 2012, I had to address 200 of my fellow residents at a celebratory dinner in the scattered community where I live (organised for us by two very good Polish friends of mine, Ela and Adam Jastzbretski) and tell them what life was like in 1952, when most of them were still unborn. I said that those who were around at the time 'look back on Coronation year as a happy time in a country full of optimism' and added, before proposing the loyal toast, that 'I guess that most of them will have, as I do, an affectionate admiration for the young woman who was then setting out on her remarkable sixty-year journey of service to the people of this country. We have been privileged to have her as our Queen.'

I conclude this chapter by reproducing, for the record, the speech I made to the BIM that caused such a stir.

60 I cannot help wondering whether Callaghan thought the Queen was talking about my Reading lecture rather than my BIM speech

It is almost exactly a year since NEDC held a well publicised all-day meeting at Chequers. At that meeting the Council unanimously agreed on the need

- to develop an agreed long-term strategy for industry
- to give higher priority to manufacturing
- to maintain greater continuity in economic policy

Despite all that has happened since, I still regard that agreement – which was embodied in a White Paper and presented to Parliament – as one of great importance for the country. We in NEDO are dedicated to making a reality of it.

At one level we can claim some modest success. The tripartite sector groups which were set up following Chequers have on the whole done well. There is an encouraging degree of commitment among the management members. The experiment of having lay convenors as well as full-time trade union officials on the groups has been generally welcomed. And the civil service contribution is more positive than in the past.

At last week's NEDC meeting we were able to report good progress on the follow-up to the sector groups' first recommendations. And while one should never underestimate the inbuilt resistance to change in British institutions, I have good hopes that when NEDC receives the definitive report on follow-up action early next year we shall have some solid achievements under our belt.

The purpose of the sector groups is to improve industrial performance through joint action by management, unions and government. To a large extent the required changes will have to be made at company and plant level and the sector groups are beginning to get down to this. But to achieve success they need a reasonably stable economic environment. This, as we all know, they have not had. In November 1975 the pound stood at over $2. Last week it was below $1.60 and the CBI survey showed a sharp drop in business confidence. At this level the aims of Chequers have not begun to be fulfilled.

For me the saddest thing about the present crisis has been its predictability. In March of this year we had a sudden and dangerous run on sterling. No one who took the trouble to consider the reasons for this can have been surprised by subsequent developments.

I am not one of those who think that the foreign exchange markets behave irrationally. It may be that at times of great uncertainty they can be unduly swayed by rumour. But the broad trends are established by intelligent men in financial institutions and large companies, who take a perceptive and informed view of the situation in different countries. In my experience a high proportion of these men are friendly to Britain: it is wrong to think of the international financial community as hostile to this country.

Many factors enter into the judgement which bankers and others make about the prospects for sterling – inflation, the balance of payments, productivity, industrial relations and so on. At the present time their attention is strongly focused on our public deficit. But the more I meet and listen to foreign observers of Britain the more convinced I become that it is not so much the absolute level of our public expenditure which concerns them as its composition. The biggest single reason for their lack of confidence is the high proportion of public borrowing required for non-productive purposes which do nothing to strengthen our economy.

This is why the reduction of the borrowing requirement by £2 billion in July did not lead to any improvement in the external value of the pound. If the whole £2 billion had come from cuts in non-productive public expenditure, the pound would in my view certainly have strengthened. But because half of it came from an additional tax on industry it failed to improve confidence. In the same way the latest run on sterling reflects a widely held view that high interest rates act as a brake on investment and exports – and that by raising the minimum lending rate to 15 per cent in order to finance the public deficit we are once again subordinating the needs of industry to those of the unproductive public sector.

There is a deeper reason why the present level of unproductive public spending is debilitating for the economy. Employment in the public services is now more protected, prospects for advancement are better and pay and conditions are generally more attractive than in manufacturing industry – especially engineering from which much of the growth in exports will have to come. This reinforces the deep-seated tendency, which our history and educational system have engendered, for administrative, professional and service employment to attract a higher share of the available talent than manufacturing industry. This bias will have to be corrected if our economy is to prosper.

For all these reasons it seems to me that an early cut in unproductive public expenditure has now become imperative. The size of the cut will need to be significant. Window-dressing reductions will not do and it would be dishonest to pretend that an increase in unemployment can be avoided. But I am not advocating savage cuts. My personal belief is that any action which convinced foreign opinion that we really accepted the need to reduce the share of national resources used in the non-productive sector – and that we would not go back on this later – would have a disproportionately good effect on sterling. It is the refusal to accept the need for this in principle which is so damaging to confidence.

Let me now turn to the other side of the equation. Cuts in public expenditure are deflationary and the last thing this country needs just now is another dose of deflation. With doubts about the prospects for world trade growing, deflationary action at home is bound to depress investment intentions and to intensify resistance on the shop floor to measures to increase productivity. A traditional deflationary package, unimaginatively applied, could take us back to the desert land we entered after July 1966 – and give a lasting setback to the effort to improve industrial performance by agreement between management and unions.

It is not a reduction in activity we need but a transfer of resources within the economy to the wealth-creating sectors. This is what the Chequers agreement was all about. In present circumstances this transfer will be extremely difficult to secure and will require economic statesmanship of a high order, both within this country and on the part of our foreign creditors. For the transfer we need is bound to involve transitional unemployment – and with over a million already out of work this is certain to be resisted (and understandably so)

George Brown unveiling the National Plan in 1967

Eric and Freda Roll with Robert McNamara, President of the World Bank

Cardinal Basil Hume

PHOTO BY ANNA ZEVILLE

With Father Wilfrid McGreal in Throwley Church

Penha de França Chapel in Madeira

With the architect, Joao Paredes, on the chapel roof

Father Bernardino overlooking Funchal Bay

The Sketch

No. 2046.—Vol. CLVIII. WEDNESDAY, APRIL 13, 1932. ONE SHILLING.

LADY PRUDENCE JELLICOE IN MID-AIR: THE SWALLOW-DIVE.

This snapshot of Lady Prudence Jellicoe, youngest daughter of Admiral Earl Jellicoe, was taken at Madeira, and shows her poised in mid-air during a perfect swallow-dive. She has dived from a rock about thirty feet above the sea at the famous Reid's Palace Hotel bathing-place. Lady Prudence has only recently learned to dive.

The eighteen-year-old Lady Prudence Jellicoe's superb dive into the Atlantic ocean in 1932 off Reid's Hotel, where I still swim (but don't dive)

With my nieces Elizabeth, Priscilla and Barbara and husbands Christopher and Michel at Reid's in 2012

With Harold Wilson and his private secretary Robin (now Lord) Butler after a good Neddy meeting in 1975

James Callaghan chairing his first Neddy meeting in 1976. The specially made round table was used so that no one group represented on the Council could be thought to be superior to the others

With Prince Philip at the Royal Thames Yacht Club in the 1980s

Speaking at the Jubilee celebrations in Throwley in 2012

With Fred and Val Smith and Doreen on the Great Wall of China

The chairman and his wife on duty at an APV function in Chicago

'I like Mr Gorbachev – we can do business together': Mrs Thatcher with the Russian leader in 1984

With Mrs Thatcher at the exhibition held during the British Month in Kiev

The McIntosh Mission to St Petersburg

With Klaus Doring and Helen Vassina at the site of the house in Ekaterinburg where Tsar Nicholas II and his family were murdered in 1918

Boris Yeltsin hands over the Russian Presidency to Vladimir Putin in 1999

PHOTO BY JOY CUTTERIDGE

The view from our house at Throwley – the church is just visible in the top left-hand corner

unless it is accompanied by clear and identifiable measures to sustain an acceptable level of growth in the manufacturing sector.

The government's freedom of action is of course heavily circumscribed by the size of the borrowing requirement, the re-emergence of inflationary pressures within our economy and the uncertain prospects for world trade. Without access to the figures one can only suggest broad areas where action might be taken to offset the deflationary effects of cuts in non-productive public expenditure.

First, increased incentives for investment. At NEDC last week we discussed the possibility of the government giving selective support to investment in manufacturing industry through a series of loans and grants broadly comparable with the Department of Industry's Accelerated Projects Scheme which expired in September. There was general support for this both at NEDC and in the Roll Committee on Finance for Investment. We were told that the government were considering it sympathetically and the Secretary of State for Industry confirmed this in Parliament yesterday.

We in NEDO strongly endorse this approach. I believe that so long as interest rates remain at around their present levels there is a strong case for what amount to interest relief grants for investment projects which will strengthen the competitive power of British industry and help to hold together the skilled labour force in our capital goods industries. This is exactly the kind of public expenditure which should be given priority. It seems to me that an outlay of around £300 million on additional help for manufacturing industry could be justified in the coming year provided offsetting savings were made in the non-productive sectors.

Secondly, imports. Over two-thirds of our imports now consist of manufactured goods. The sector groups' reports showed that there is great scope for import substitution through closer collaboration between industrial purchasers and suppliers of capital goods and components in this country. The fall in the value of the pound is an inducement to save imports and no doubt large industrial purchasers will normally buy from abroad only if no satisfactory product is available from British sources. But how many industrial purchasers who are faced with this situation actively seek to create a new British source through co-operation with potential suppliers? The evidence collected by the sector groups suggests that very little of this is done. I suggest that this is an area where an initiative from the larger companies could produce worthwhile results.

As to other forms of import restraint I am entirely opposed to general import controls since – quite apart from the risks of retaliation – they simply buttress inefficiency and delay the improvements in design, delivery and so on which the sector groups show to be so badly needed. Where a sector of industry is already making a co-ordinated effort to improve performance, for example within the framework of an Industry Act scheme, these considerations may not apply. If the sector is important to the national economy the case for containing import penetration for a defined period, to maintain capacity in being while restructuring is carried out, need not perhaps be rejected out of hand.

Thirdly, taxation. The prospect that the public borrowing requirement should be reduced by raising taxes frankly appals me. To raise indirect taxes would do nothing to encourage the transfer of resources to the productive sector and would greatly add to the difficulties of maintaining pay restraint through the winter. To increase direct taxation would be unthinkable. It is quite clear – and well understood by foreigners – that current levels of direct taxation are a serious drag on improved industrial performance. The right direction for taxation to move in Britain is downwards. A modest reduction in direct taxation at the lower end of the scale could help to improve productivity, contain inflation, sustain growth and strengthen confidence at home and abroad.

I would like to be able to end on a cheerful note. But the truth is that we are in a very difficult situation and it does no good to try and minimise it. One of the reasons why we are in our present difficulties is that too many people have shut their eyes to what was happening around them – and over-optimistic official forecasts have encouraged them in this.

But we should not forget that we have one great asset. It has always been a characteristic of Britain that when times get really difficult opinion tends to converge rather than polarise. I believe this characteristic is as strong as it ever was. The right course is to build on it; to avoid getting impaled on political or economic dogma of any variety; and to develop broad policies for steering the economy through its present difficulties which will command general – even if reluctant – support in the country as a whole. Provided that in parallel we press on vigorously with the structural changes and improvements in performance with which we in NEDO are especially concerned, then the prospect in two years' time – when North Sea oil will mean that we are running a balance of payments surplus – could be vastly different.

–CHAPTER FIFTEEN–

THE PRIVATE SECTOR

Directors General of Neddy were not appointed for a fixed term; my three predecessors had served for four, five and two years respectively. As time went on, it looked increasingly likely that Jim Callaghan would call a general election in autumn 1978, by which time I would have been in the post for over five years, and I decided I should go before then. In the event he decided not to call the election which most people thought he would have won in October 1978 but to wait until the following year by which time the 'winter of discontent' had made his defeat inevitable.

The general election of May 1979 marked the end of a decade of decline, confusion and economic failure which had taken the country to the brink of economic collapse. It also closed a distinctive chapter of post-war British history, which included the Attlee government's social reforms, the independence of India, the brief life of 'one nation' Conservatism and our accession to the European Community. As leadership passed to a new generation, with new ideas and values, North Sea oil began to come ashore and ushered in a period of ten or more years of political stability (though not of consensus) which I had so often argued was a precondition of our return to economic strength. Whatever its other pluses and minuses, this made it an interesting time to join the private sector where I had for a long time wanted to spend the last lap of my working life. I didn't of course know then that this would last another twenty years.

I told Douglas Allen what I had in mind. I also told the Prime Minister, who spoke pleasantly about my time in Neddy but made no attempt to dissuade me. Then I had a word with my old friend and boss Eric Roll who – as chairman of Warburgs, a member of the Court of the Bank of England and an independent member of NEDC – was now a City grandee and would be a good source of advice if I needed it. Not long afterwards I received a call from Siegmund Warburg and went to see him in his office. He was full of compliments about the independent line I had taken in Neddy, said he liked non-conformists and pressed me to join the merchant bank that bore his name. By this time Siegmund was seventy-five, with his main home in Switzerland; when I became a director of Warburgs in the following year, with a commitment to spend half my time on its affairs, he no longer held any official post in the bank and I never got to know him well. But the firm still bore the stamp of his unusual personality and – control freak that he was – he kept in touch with every detail of its activity.

The bank he created, in collaboration with Henry Grunfeld, another refugee from Hitler's Germany, was an extraordinary phenomenon. The two men, whose talents and personalities perfectly complemented one another, went into business together in Britain before the war: but it was not until 1957 that the firm they established was able to become a pukka merchant bank. This only became possible when they acquired Seligman Brothers, a small but long-established firm which brought as its dowry a seat on the Accepting Houses Committee and, with it, admission to the City's magic circle. A mere twenty years later Warburgs was arguably the leading British merchant bank, with an international reputation for innovative methods and dedicated professionalism. Siegmund and Grunfeld achieved this remarkable outcome by the care with which they recruited their senior staff, who were mostly clever ex-public school boys with outgoing personalities; by Grunfeld's exceptional banking skills; and by Siegmund's ability to indoctrinate everyone in the business with his own vision of what a merchant bank should be and how it should be run.

As it seemed to me, Siegmund's management philosophy rested on three main pillars. The first was that he and a handful of senior directors kept in touch with everything the rest of the staff were doing. This was achieved by personal contact, by frequent internal meetings and by a simple mechanism through which significant correspondence was briefly summarised and circulated to all directors every day. (This was modelled on an earlier tradition of the partners in most merchant banks opening the mail together every morning.) The second was that the bank's relationship with its established clients had to be given top priority, even at the expense of profit. The third was that everyone must maintain the highest standards of integrity in their work and do nothing that could endanger the bank's reputation. Failure to observe this principle would require the miscreant to walk the plank.

I found the bank a congenial and stimulating place to work. The directors were all thoroughly civilised people and the English public school culture was leavened by an important sprinkling of people from other (mainly European) countries. Inevitably, in such a talented group there were some prima donnas – indeed, to some extent they were all prima donnas. No doubt there were strong rivalries among the younger, up-and-coming staff of which I was not necessarily aware, but virtually all the work was done by teams rather than by individuals and Siegmund put great weight on effective team-working in the bank (not least because he knew that there would always be someone on the team who would be willing to tell him what was really going on within it).

When I went to work there I was given a desk in a room which I shared with a much younger director, Michael Orr, who held a senior position in the corporate finance department of the bank. It proved, for me, to be an excellent arrangement. Michael was a delightful man – highly intelligent and a thorough professional like all his peers – and seemed quite happy to act as mentor to an older man who (despite my years in Whitehall working at the interface between industry and government) was woefully ignorant not only of the idiosyncratic ways of Warburgs but of the intricacies of company balance sheets and rights issues which were the daily pabulum of merchant bankers. Michael himself was not one of the ex-public schoolboy brigade. He went to a grammar school and sometimes likened Warburg's success in outdoing most of the old style merchant bankers of the magic circle and the 'Governor's eyebrows' culture to the victory of the grammar school boys over their public school counterparts. Later in life he paid me the compliment of saying that he thought I really belonged in the grammar school camp.

To begin with there were aspects of the Warburg culture which I found irksome. Siegmund was a passionate believer in graphology and, as someone in his fifties, with quite wide experience and some achievements behind me, I thought it a little unseemly to be asked to submit a sample of my handwriting to the Swiss lady expert on whom he relied to see what character defects – or strengths, I suppose – it revealed. But I swallowed my pride and did as I was told and, as I never heard any more about it, I presume I passed whatever test was involved. More seriously, I was irritated at the outset by a number of the procedures which were part of the overarching system designed to enable Siegmund and his senior colleagues to monitor what I and my counterparts throughout the bank were up to. But as I came to understand why these checks had been put in place I willingly accepted them. All in all, I had a huge admiration for the way Siegmund put his vision into effect in the management of the bank. His success in maintaining the high standards of integrity, professionalism and internal discipline which were his hallmark, while at the same time keeping his ambitious and talented colleagues fully motivated, was truly impressive.

In 1982 Siegmund died; in 1995 S. G. Warburg & Co. was taken over by a large Swiss competitor; and in 2002, as part of a rebranding exercise, the Warburg name ceased to exist. I had by then retired and was not privy to what led to these developments, but it is difficult to avoid the conclusion that in their handling of the bank's affairs in the aftermath of the 'Big Bang' of 1986 (which completely altered the structure and character of world banking) those in charge did not quite live up to the high standards Siegmund had instilled in them. It also seems reasonable to believe that if Warburgs had been able to retain its separate identity (even if not its complete independence) and its founder's management philosophy, some of the excesses which have disfigured British banking in recent years would have been avoided.

It was through Warburgs that I became chairman of APV. In 1981 Peter Benson, a chartered accountant who had completed twenty-five years in the company, first as finance director and later as an effective chairman, was due to retire. Geoffrey Seligman, a distant cousin of the company's founder and deputy chairman of Warburgs (who were APV's long-standing bankers) put my name forward as a possible successor. After a meeting with the board I was offered and accepted the job, which gave me eight years of hard but thoroughly rewarding work.

The founder, Dr Richard Seligman, was an anglophile German who studied engineering at Heidelberg, married a British woman, Hilda MacDowell, and settled in England. My old friend, Madron Seligman, was their third son. Richard founded APV (as the Aluminium Plate and Vessel Company) in 1910 and subsequently invented the plate heat exchanger, which revolutionised heat transfer between liquids and became an essential part of many industrial processes. An example of his heat exchanger is, I believe, still on show in the Science Museum in London.

Until the 1950s APV was a family-controlled company, run first by Richard and later by his eldest son, Peter (who was one of the British pioneers of skiing in Switzerland and became chairman of the Ski Club of Great Britain). It then became a public company, employing around 11,000 people, with headquarters at Crawley in Sussex, a substantial presence in Europe, North America, Australia and South

Africa, and a network of sales and service companies in Asia and Latin America. Its business was the design and manufacture of sophisticated plant and machinery used in the processing of food, beverages, pharmaceuticals and other products where quality and hygiene were of paramount importance. Worldwide, it was the second most important supplier of this type of equipment, after – and some way behind – the Swedish company Alfa-Laval. Under the Seligmans its expansion had been steady but gradual; almost all the overseas subsidiaries were indigenous and several had been family businesses whose owners were willing to sell their companies but stayed on to run them as part of the APV group. The long period of family ownership still had an influence on the company's business culture when I joined, but there were some among both its managers and shareholders who were keen to grow the business to a size which more nearly matched Alfa-Laval's.

APV was a decentralised company in which the management of the various subsidiaries had a good deal of autonomy. One of my first tasks was to get to know the senior people throughout the group and to see and be seen at their main factories and offices. As soon as I had covered the principal units in Britain, I planned a travel programme to visit the main overseas companies and meet the people running them. They were a good team, many with long service in the company, who looked as though they would be capable, under strong leadership, of managing a more rapidly expanding business. However, it became clear that the Chief Executive, who had been recruited from outside the group a couple of years before I came on board, was not the right man for the job. His Harvard Business School approach did not sit comfortably with APV's business culture and he departed early in 1984.

His successor, promoted from within the group, was an Australian, Fred Smith, who had worked for some years in the United States and had the direct, informal style for which his countrymen are noted. He also had two qualities we thought the post required: he knew a great deal about the industries APV served and he was a first class motivator of people of different nationalities. Fred was a very effective chief executive and a good human being; we worked well together and became friends as well as colleagues.

Trading conditions in the United Kingdom were difficult in the early 1980s as the Chancellor, Sir Geoffrey Howe, took forceful action in successive budgets to repair the damage caused by the inflationary mayhem of the previous decade. By the time Fred took over, the economy was showing some signs of recovery and he put in hand a rationalisation programme which quite quickly began to show results. This was just as well because early in 1986 we received an aggressively hostile takeover bid from a diversified company which was known chiefly as a manufacturer of diving equipment. The bid was plainly opportunistic but the terms offered to our shareholders were generous and the general opinion in the City was that the bid would succeed.

It was clear to me that the long-term interest of our shareholders and employees would be better served if we remained independent and the board shared this view. We accordingly decided to resist the attempted takeover with all our might. Fred Smith handed over day-to-day responsibility for managing the group to the man in charge of our US operations, Don Hefner, an able and experienced American who moved to London for the duration. This left Fred free to join me in working full time on the bid. After a great deal of hard work – and ably advised by Piers von Simson of Warburgs and Anthony Forbes of our stockbrokers Cazenoves (two of the best people in the business) – we were successful. Some said that what clinched this was a circular we sent to our shareholders in which I said that the only synergy between the bidder and APV that I could think of was that the two companies combined could supply an underwater dairy, if anyone wanted one. The City liked it and, whether for this or weightier reasons, our shareholders backed the board and rejected the proposed takeover.

The APV board was a strong one with which it was a great pleasure to work. I firmly believed that a company with large international interests should always include some directors from countries other than Britain – a view which was not very widely shared in those days. During my time as chairman we recruited two distinguished non-executive directors from overseas: Sir Russel Madigan, a leading figure in the Australian business community and a director of the international mining group RTZ, and Hugh Kraijenhof, a wise Dutch industrialist who was chairman of the supervisory board of Akzo, with directorships in the USA and Britain, and was a tower of strength to me in times of difficulty. By the time I retired, three of our executive directors, responsible for managing the company's largest subsidiaries, were foreign nationals from the USA, Denmark and Germany. The non-executive directors also included Sir Charles Reece, the research director of ICI, Astley Whittall, an industrialist who was also chairman of the Engineering Industry Training Board, and Ernest Sharp, an accountant with wide experience of the food industry. All made very positive contributions to the board's deliberations.

The generous terms offered by the bidders and the belief that the bid would probably be successful led to a sharp rise in APV's share price. Following its defeat the onus was on us to show that we could run the business well enough to justify the market's increased valuation of the company. The most attractive option for expansion seemed to us to be to join forces with an old established British company of good repute, Baker Perkins. This was based in Peterborough and had a somewhat smaller turnover but more employees than APV. It was a world leader in the design and manufacture of bakery equipment which would perfectly complement APV's product range. I made it clear that, as long as I was chairman I would not agree to the company making a hostile takeover bid. I had long believed that such takeovers, which were very fashionable at that time, were a thoroughly unsatisfactory way of restructuring British industry. My view was that they had a hugely damaging effect on morale in the company taken over, made the process of integrating it into the bidder's business very difficult and often led to a drift of good people away from it to seek employment elsewhere. In my experience hostile bids usually have less to do with industrial logic than with the personality of the bidder.

When the board agreed that we should try to achieve a consensual takeover or merger with Baker Perkins, I was about to set out on a visit which both the Chief Executive of Baker Perkins, Mike Smith, and I were making to China, as members of a British trade mission led by my friend, the former Cabinet minister, Lord Jellicoe. (This was a remarkable visit, made especially memorable by the fact that the Queen, who was paying a State visit to China, graciously allowed the mission to entertain their Chinese guests on board the royal yacht *Britannia* in Shanghai, while she and Prince Philip were in Beijing.) I took the opportunity to discuss our proposal privately with Mike Smith during a walk along the Bund in Shanghai, knowing that this would give him time and space to think it over before he got home and discussed it with his chairman and the board of Baker Perkins.

Contrary to all the theoretical rules of negotiating behaviour, I told Mike Smith that we would not make a hostile bid for his company: our wish was to achieve an agreed takeover or merger which each side considered to be in its own interest and if we couldn't get this we would drop the idea. (This reflected the lesson I had learned from Frank Lee during the British/Australian trade negotiations described in Chapter 8.) I am happy to say that an agreed merger was subsequently negotiated (again with excellent professional support from von Simson and his team) to the mutual benefit of both companies' shareholders.

Our next big acquisition was in many ways the most interesting we made under my chairmanship. In 1987 we learned that a large Danish conglomerate wanted to dispose of a subsidiary company (named Pasilac) specialising in the design and manufacture of machinery for processing milk and other liquids, which formed the core of APV's own business. It was clear that the extra capacity, product range and skilled personnel that Pasilac would bring with it would provide us with an immediate opportunity to expand in the way we were looking for. We were able to negotiate the purchase for a satisfactory price. I no longer have access to the statistical records for this acquisition but it was big enough to make us, for a time, the largest British investors in manufacturing plant in Denmark.

Pasilac's manufacturing facilities were spread over a number of smallish factories in Jutland and in one of

Denmark's many islands. In the months after the change of ownership, I also made it my business to visit the mayors of all the townships where the factories were located in order to introduce APV and let them know that we were responsible employers with a proper concern for the communities in which we operated. This approach was well received and well worth the effort, and it was always a pleasure to visit factories in Denmark, which must be the cleanest and best kept in the world.

In the course of the next few years Doreen and I made a number of visits to Denmark, a country we both came to like very much. Two royal occasions stand out clearly in my memory. The first was an open air performance of *Hamlet* with Kenneth Branagh playing the Prince, which took place at Elsinore in the presence of Queen Margrethe. As luck would have it, it poured with rain almost continuously throughout the evening – so much so that by half way through the actors were wearing anoraks over their stage costumes. We were told that in the interval Branagh had asked the Queen if they should call the show off because of the weather: but she said she was enjoying it so much that she hoped they would carry on. The Queen was in fact the only person in the grounds who had a temporary roof over her head: but though soaked to the skin, we didn't mind – we were simply pleased to be present at this historic event.

The second occasion was a dinner at the British Embassy for the Queen and the Prince Consort. Our good friend

Peter Unwin, the Ambassador at the time, was about to retire and the Queen had let it be known that, if invited to the Embassy for a farewell dinner, she would be happy to accept. Peter and his wife Monica accordingly arranged a dinner at their residence to which they invited eight guests who lived in Copenhagen and eight, including us, from Britain. It was a most enjoyable evening and an occasion to remember.

Another excellent spin-off from our acquisition of Pasilac was that its managing director, Alf Duch-Pedersen, came with it. Alf was a very able and congenial man, who joined the APV board as an executive director after the takeover and played a very effective role in the group. Some years after I retired he left APV to become head of Den Danske Bank – a prestigious post which I am told ranks in many Danish minds as the third most important in the country, after the monarch and the Prime Minister.

Doreen threw herself enthusiastically into the job of being the chairman's wife and we did a good deal of travelling together. I strongly believe that this is an important part of a non-executive chairman's role, which can do a lot to motivate executive management, especially overseas. I believe that, if she is willing to do so, a chairman's wife can play a very valuable part in strengthening managers' loyalty to a company, which is of great importance in an international group, where it is all too easy for the staff of outlying subsidiaries (and their wives) to feel unappreciated by the faceless bureaucrats at headquarters.

Looking back on those years, I am in no doubt that our joint visits, particularly to the United States, South Africa and Australia were as useful as they were enjoyable. On one visit to Australia, however, we managed to see the trial races for the America's Cup in a smallish tug off Fremantle, which APV's local manager had hired to take us and some of his most important customers out. It was a bright sunny day but the ocean swell (the famous Fremantle doctor) was very heavy and the only people on board who were not seasick were Doreen, myself and the local manager. I imagine that from then onwards he always referred to me as the chairman who lost him his best customers.

When I retired, Fred Smith wrote a generous article for the APV house magazine about our time with the company which, perhaps self-indulgently, I reproduce below.

> Ronnie came to APV at a time when it was suffering from a prolonged period of declining returns on capital employed and earnings per share.
>
> He supported a great deal of internal reorganisation which included the sale of certain non-core subsidiaries. By 1985 the company was back on track with a doubling of profit over the preceding year. At that time the share price was still low and APV was vulnerable to attack by a predator – that occurred in 1986 when an unwelcome bid for the company was made.
>
> Ronnie McIntosh is an extraordinary chairman. Through his ability he commands respect and loyalty, and generates action and

enthusiasm in others. One of his fine achievements at APV came in 1986 when we fought off the hostile bid.

Initially, neither the City or the press gave APV much of a chance of remaining independent, quoting the bid as 'a knockout blow'. The chairman rallied and with his knowledge of the City introduced a plan with such good effect that the bidder retreated in defeat and the new APV was created under his chairmanship. His command of public relations is unsurpassed, and he has always had a continuing dialogue with the shareholders which played an important part in the company remaining independent.

A new era opened for APV. Sir Ronald and his team had made the City increase its awareness of APV, and the company's shares were re-rated substantially upwards. By then the management's perception was sharpened even further as to where the company should go in the future.

A four-year plan was introduced and an acquisition strategy vigorously pursued, with Sir Ronald's insistence on agreed, non-hostile bids. In 1986 APV acquired a controlling interest in Rosista, providing an outlet for its products in West Germany, and access to a range of high-integrity valves for the beverage industry. Three important acquisitions were made in the US, providing important additions to the group's ice-cream range of machinery. In Britain, W&C Pantin came into the group with specialised equipment for mechanical handling for breweries and escalators for public transport which, incidentally, have been of particular interest to Sir Ronald, who has been jokingly referred to as our 'centre of excellence' by London Transport.

A milestone, but not the end of the road, was reached in 1987 with the acquisition of Baker Perkins, which was seen as highly complementary to APV's traditional business, with hardly any overlap between the two companies. The group then had sales of over £700 million, 14,000 employees and 20 principal production sites around the world.

Soon afterwards, Pasilac became part of the APV group and Sir Ronald led the group into a classic period of post-takeover integration, with the 200 constituent subsidiaries in APV, Baker Perkins and Pasilac trimmed down to nine principal subsidiaries, complete with a new corporate image, and all implemented in only a few months. As Sir Ronald hands over the reins, he leaves APV in better shape than at any time in its history.

In expressing my thanks to him for his outstanding service to APV, I also reflect on his devoted wife, Lady Doreen. She has been a tireless companion who has endured many long trips to APV outposts around the world. Doreen has always been a keen supporter of everything that Ronnie does and her influence has provided a great deal of the stamina that he is noted for.

–CHAPTER SIXTEEN–

RUSSIA

RUSSIA – 'A RIDDLE wrapped in a mystery inside an enigma', in Churchill's famous phrase – played an important part in the final years of my working life. Although I had already been to Moscow a couple of times, my close association with the country began in 1984 when Mikhail Gorbachev paid his first visit to London – a visit made famous by Margaret Thatcher's remark to the press at the end of their Downing Street meeting: 'I like Mr Gorbachev: we can do business together.'

Gorbachev was then only the second highest-ranking member of the Soviet Politburo, which was chaired by the ailing Konstantin Chernenko, the third successive member of the Communist gerontocracy (after Brezhnev and Andropov) to serve as General Secretary. The Soviet economy was at the time in a state of crisis, the country was demoralised and it was becoming clear that fundamental reforms were required if the world's second superpower was to avoid a potentially terminal decline.

As a charismatic and intelligent representative of a younger generation, Gorbachev was seen by many as a possible successor to Chernenko. But conservative forces in Moscow still held most of the reins of power and it was by no means certain that he would be able to defeat their candidate, Viktor Grishin – described by the *Washington Post* correspondent Robert Kaiser (whose father Philip had been my friend and contemporary at Balliol and later minister at the American embassy in London) as 'a walking embodiment of the personal and political values of the Brezhnev era: ponderous, predictable and deeply involved in corruption'.

The principal function laid on by the British government for Gorbachev's visit was a luncheon at Hampton Court, hosted by the Foreign Secretary Geoffrey Howe. This was a historic event and I was delighted to be present at it. My pleasure was all the greater when I found myself sitting next to the playwright Michael Frayn, whose comedy *Noises Off* (one of the funniest to reach the London stage in my lifetime) was playing to full houses at the Savoy Theatre. Gorbachev's visit, on which he was accompanied by his equally charismatic wife Raisa – a most untypical partner for a Politburo grandee – was a great success and his election to the top job some months later was widely welcomed in Britain.

As the era of *glasnost* and *perestroika* began, British industry's interest in the Russian market – and my own involvement in it as chairman of APV – grew apace. It so happened that in 1987 (as described in Chapter 16) APV made an important acquisition in Denmark which opened up significant new opportunities for expanding sales to Russia. The Danish company we acquired had put a big effort into marketing its products in the Soviet Union and had a well-staffed office in Moscow. This provided a useful basis for developing business with Russia for the rest of the group's products and I took an early opportunity to visit the Moscow office and to get to know the staff and their most important local contacts. Among these was the Danish Ambassador to Russia, an experienced diplomat, Rudi Thorning-Petersen, who ended his career as a well respected Ambassador in London, where he and his wife Brita became good friends of Doreen's and mine. Brita told a story of how, when the Danish Foreign Minister stayed with them in Moscow and asked her where she would like her husband to be posted when the time came to move on, she replied: 'As our last posting before Russia was in Saudi Arabia, could it please be in a country where I don't have to learn another alphabet?' As someone who, despite my many visits to Russia, has never felt completely at ease with Cyrillic script, I thought she had a point.

Following this visit to Moscow I took a close interest in the changes taking place in Russia under Gorbachev and in my own company's business there. There were frequent food shortages at the time, which caused widespread discontent, and I soon learned that the food sector (in which APV was involved as a supplier of specialised machinery) was in a deplorable state and in urgent need of modernisation. The lack of up-to-date processing plants and the appalling inefficiencies in the storage and distribution of food led to huge waste and misdirection of resources. It was clear that there was little point in building a new dairy here, modernising an old sugar mill there and a bakery somewhere else if there was no infrastructure to get the product in reasonable condition from the farm to the consumer. It also became obvious that if the losses occurring in the system, which were estimated to be as much as 40 per cent of total farm output, could be eliminated the country would not have a food shortage at all.

The food sector is one in which British companies have considerable strengths and my increasing knowledge of conditions in Russia led me to float the idea, in discussion with two or three companies which APV knew well, that we should form a consortium (consortia were at that time very popular with the Soviet bureaucracy) to help the Russian authorities in specific regions to develop an integrated food chain – storage, processing, packaging, transport and distribution – of the kind that was commonplace in the West.

This suggestion was favourably received and in due course seven well-known companies – five from the food industry, together with a builder and a bank[61] – formed the British

61 Allied Lyons, APV, Booker Tate, United Biscuits, Vestey Group, Taylor Woodrow and Morgan Grenfell

Food Consortium to implement it. In a characteristically British way this was really more of a club than a consortium. It had no corporate structure or financial resources of its own, though it introduced certain legal safeguards when we received support from the British taxpayer under the government's foreign aid programme. Its strength lay in the fact that all its members were like-minded companies of repute which had a long-term interest in the Russian market, and the enthusiasm which the young company executives who did the real work brought to its activities meant that the BFC served its purpose well.

The consortium, of which I became chairman, received strong support from Her Majesty's Government. In its first year the BFC concluded an agreement with the Council of Ministers of the Ukrainian SSR to send a team of specialists to investigate the storage, processing and distribution of meat, milk, fruit, vegetables and sugar in the Kiev region. This was signed in Kiev in the presence of Margaret Thatcher, who was visiting Ukraine to support a British month held there in June 1990.

The British month was a colourful and well-run event, with an exhibition put on by British companies keen to do business in Ukraine, including the members of the BFC. It was attended at its opening by the Princess Royal and the band of the Coldstream Guards and at its close by Margaret Thatcher and English National Opera. It is perhaps worth recounting a little-known story of the final night. During the interval in ENO's performance of Handel's opera *Xerxes* (which I thought a very unsuitable choice for a Russian city as all the male parts were sung by counter-tenors) the British visitors withdrew to an ante-room for a reception hosted by the Mayor of Kiev. I returned to my seat before the others in time to see a balloon descend from the upper reaches of the theatre and land neatly in the Prime Minister's box. On it was painted 'Kill the Poll Tax'. This was believed to be the work of an enterprising British student who was living temporarily in Kiev. With their usual efficiency the KGB quickly despatched the balloon and so far as I know Mrs Thatcher (for whom the slogan might well have touched a raw nerve at that particular time) never saw or knew of it.

Kiev is a fine city with a grand position on the banks of the river Dnieper. I spent my spare time exploring the scene of the street-fighting which is vividly described in *The White Guard*, Bulgakov's classic novel about the Russian Civil War. Ukraine, through which Christianity came to Russia, has a proud history but it seemed to me to have slipped during Soviet rule into a state of provincial torpor. In contrast to some of their Moscow counterparts, the officials with whom we dealt were very friendly and seemed genuinely eager to learn from the West: but Moscow's dominant position was so deeply ingrained in the system that the calibre of the senior people in Kiev was, I thought, comparable with that of county councillors in England rather than with Westminster MPs or Whitehall officials.

There was strong support in some parts of the country (though not in parts of the east where the bulk of the population were ethnic Russians) for greater use of the Ukrainian language and there was a reasonably vigorous movement in favour of national independence. But many of the people I met seemed a bit bewildered at the prospect of independence and uncertain about the country's ability to make a success of it. However, we were living in a period of change – less than two years later the Soviet Union was dissolved, Ukraine became an independent sovereign state and Margaret Thatcher ceased to be Prime Minister of the United Kingdom.

I was no longer involved in Ukraine's affairs at the time of the 'Orange Revolution' of 2004 but developments in the current century seem to bear out the mood I had detected in the 1990s. The problems caused by the historic fault line between western and eastern Ukraine are still very much alive and I find it hard to believe that they will be sufficiently resolved in the foreseeable future to prevent the country's eventual partition.

[The two preceding paragraphs were written in 2013, before President Putin's annexation of Crimea and the fighting in Donetsk and other cities of eastern Ukraine. I have left them unaltered because they show that what happened in 2014 should not have come as a surprise to anyone who knew Ukraine. The question I ask myself now is: did the European policy-makers in Brussels (the capital of a country whose ethnic, linguistic and religious differences are uncannily similar to those of Ukraine) not know that any Russian government – and certainly President Putin's – was likely to resist with the utmost vigour any attempt to bring the strategically located state of Ukraine, through which all Russia's invaders in the last couple of centuries have passed, into the orbit of the European Union and therefore, by extension, of NATO? For anyone with a knowledge of history this was not difficult to foresee.]

The BFC team did a good job in Kiev. They established excellent relations with their Ukrainian counterparts and their recommendations were all accepted by the authorities in Kiev. Two BFC experts went to Kiev to supervise the introduction of the changes they proposed and a number of Ukrainians visited Britain for training. I was pleased to receive a letter from the Foreign Secretary, Douglas Hurd, congratulating us 'on all the British Food Consortium is doing to bring some sense into food distribution in the Ukraine' and going on to say that our initiative struck him as a model of what technical assistance should be.

In the years following Ukraine's independence, relations between our two countries were very good. When President Kravchuk of Ukraine and his wife visited the UK in 1993 John Major hosted a friendly lunch for them in Downing Street which Doreen and I attended; and I chaired a CBI conference at which both the President and the deputy Prime Minister of Ukraine spoke. Their contrasting styles illustrated the ambivalence of the post-Communist governments of those days. As I recorded at the time,

> The President's address was quite positive, though I suspect that his attachment to the market economy is not very profound. Mr Penzenik on the other hand spoke with great conviction about his government's commitment to privatisation and the free market; his own commitment to reform and democracy is obviously sincere but he is probably well ahead of most of his colleagues in this.

In the course of 1991 the food shortages that had been plaguing the former Soviet Union for a decade or more became acute. St Petersburg was particularly affected and there were some (not entirely implausible) fears that the city, which had suffered so grievously during its wartime siege, might see a recurrence of deaths from starvation in the coming winter. The British and other European governments considered what they might do to help and John Major's Cabinet decided to despatch an experienced team to St Petersburg to assess the situation and recommend remedial measures. The Prime Minister asked me to lead this team, which became known as the McIntosh Mission. The Minister of Agriculture John Gummer (now Lord Deben) assembled a strong group from the food and agriculture industries for the purpose and we were given to understand that the government had provisionally earmarked £20 million for whatever emergency help we recommended.

On our arrival in St Petersburg we discussed the current situation with a series of experts in and around the city and then had a two-hour meeting with Anatoli Sobchak, the newly-elected Mayor of St Petersburg. Sobchak was the first elected mayor in Russia's history; he was a hugely charismatic figure who had leapt to prominence as a member of the Soviet Union's fledgling parliament in 1989 and quickly became the second most popular politician nationally after Gorbachev. He was a most unusual figure, a liberal-minded former Professor of Economics who had never been a member of the Communist Party and had a command of English that made an interpreter superfluous at our meeting.

I found him an immensely attractive character, whose outgoing personality and open-minded attitude boded well, as I thought, for the new Russia. At the end of our meeting he urged me to appear on television with him that evening for one of his weekly broadcasts to his fellow citizens – something I would have been more than happy to do but was obliged to decline as we had to leave for Moscow straight after our meeting. It was all very different from my previous experiences in the old Russia.

Given my impression of Sobchak on this first encounter, which I think all my colleagues shared, I was greatly saddened when in 1996 he was accused of bribery and had to leave the country in humiliating circumstances. Three years later when Vladimir Putin (who had been a member of Sobchak's mayoral team in St Petersburg) became Prime Minister, the charges against him were dropped and he returned to Russia. However, he died in 2000 and, so far as I know, the truth about the events in which he was said to have been involved has never been established one way or the other.

My first reaction to the charges against him was one of utter disbelief. But there is no doubt that corruption was rife among top apparatchiks in the Soviet Union in which Sobchak grew up and, as I learned during the time I spent in post-communist Russia, it increased exponentially during the Yeltsin years. So, human nature being what it is, it is not impossible that Sobchak was involved in some form of wrong-doing. However, I cannot help feeling that with his death Russia lost a potential leader who could have made a major contribution to its transition to democratic rule.

For the McIntosh Mission this was, of course, all in the future. On our return we made our recommendations to

Her Majesty's Government which accepted them all. Our most important proposal was not one we had envisaged making when we set out. We learned during our visit that St Petersburg was experiencing an acute shortage of animal feed. Plans were therefore already being made to slaughter all the cattle and use the meat to feed the people. While this might have eliminated the food shortage for several months it would clearly have had appalling long-term consequences. Our core recommendation to the British government was therefore that they should make £20 million available for the purchase of emergency imports of cattle feed to keep the cows alive through the winter and beyond – and this is what happened. I think it was a sensible answer to the question that was put to us.

In 2012 I visited St Petersburg again, on holiday with my nieces and their husbands. As we walked along the Nevsky Prospekt it seemed to me that the young Russians we saw, born after the fall of Communism, were very different from the dour citizens (many with peaked faces because they had lived through the wartime siege) whom I had encountered on my last visit in the 1990s. This time, as they fussed over their iPhones and tablets, they seemed to me exactly like their counterparts in Milan, Dusseldorf or Bristol. This could have been naive wishful thinking on my part, but I don't think it was. Everything I saw and heard on this latest visit led me to believe that, with all its faults and problems, the post-communist era represents such a complete break with what went before it that Russia's rulers will find it difficult to persuade its people to accept a prolonged return to an authoritarian way of life – a life which is quite different from what they know exists in western Europe. I realise, of course, that St Petersburg is not representative of Russia as a whole and that in any case Russia's history sets it apart from other European countries: but I can only say that I left St Petersburg on that occasion feeling more optimistic than I had been on my arrival and I believe there were some solid grounds for this. Time will tell: we must expect the transition from seventy years of Communism to take at least another generation to settle down. Meanwhile, three cheers for Pussy Riot.[62]

In the years following the fall of the Berlin Wall in 1989 the business community in Britain, as well as the general public, followed the unfolding events in the former Soviet Union with keen interest. As a result, what we were doing in the British Food Consortium became quite well known, especially after Mrs Thatcher's visit to Kiev. One man who noted its formation with particular interest was Bruce Beharrell of Amersham International, a bioscience and pharmaceutical

62 For an illuminating account of the activities of this remarkable group of young women see Masha Gessen, *Words Will Break Cement* (Granta Publications, 2014)

company involved in nuclear medicine, which had been spun off from the Atomic Energy Authority in Britain. Amersham had a close relationship with a Russian nuclear establishment in Chelyabinsk – a closed city in the Urals to which access was rigorously controlled because of the nature of its work. Beharrell, who was responsible for his company's business with Russia, was a good lateral thinker and judged that the BFC concept might be usefully applied to the healthcare sector. Discussions subsequently took place among a powerful group of companies working in this field and in a remarkably short space of time the British Healthcare Consortium (BHCC) was established in April 1992. Once again Her Majesty's Government was very supportive and the consortium was formally inaugurated at Lancaster House during President Yeltsin's visit to London some months later.

The founders' vision for the BHCC was an ambitious one and its structure was more formal than the BFC's. It had a membership of six companies from the healthcare sector, plus a construction company, a bank and the consultancy arm of the National Health Service,[63] supported by a small and efficient staff in London. The founders had also taken what seemed to me to be an intelligent decision to keep clear of Moscow and St Petersburg, which they thought would be swarming with international competitors seek-

63 Amersham, Glaxo, Smiths Industries, Zeneca, Wellcome, Vickers, Miller Group, Moscow Narodny Bank (London) and NHS Overseas Enterprises

ing business in the emerging market of post-Communist Russia. Instead, they set up an office in Ekaterinburg, the capital of the Urals Region and within easy reach of the main centres of economic activity in Siberia.

Their strategy was to offer Russian healthcare authorities set up under the old Soviet system a comprehensive service that would help them to adapt to the requirements of the market economy to which the country was now committed. To achieve this the consortium planned to provide a package comprising the supply of pharmaceuticals and medical equipment, hospital design and construction, consultancy services, training in Britain for doctors and other healthcare personnel, and expert help with managing their financial relations with the outside world. I thought their plans were well laid and when they invited me to be the consortium's first chairman I was happy to accept.

The company executives with whom I was to work, most of whom were not much more than half my age, were a pleasant, well-motivated group and were as interested as I was to be involved in the historic changes that were taking place in Russia. As things turned out in the turbulent conditions of the Yeltsin years, we were not able to achieve all we set out to do: but it was fascinating to be first-hand witnesses of one of the twentieth century's most dramatic episodes and I count the five years I spent with the consortium as among the most interesting of my long career.

Soon after I joined the consortium we paid a full-scale visit to the Urals. The first stop was Ufa, the capital of Bashkortostan, a smallish enclave originally settled by a group from Genghis Khan's westbound horde and a so-called autonomous republic in Soviet times. It was here that we made our first presentation of the new healthcare package described above. It was made to a large audience and seemed to arouse a great deal of interest. Foreign visitors from the West were then a rare sight in Ufa, which at that time was known, if at all, for being the birthplace of Mr Kalashnikov, the eponymous gunsmith. After the presentation I had a conversation with a delightful man who came up and introduced himself (through an interpreter) as Dr Gordon, a surgeon at a local hospital. He spoke no English but told me he was a descendant of one of the numerous Scots who had come to Russia a couple of centuries earlier to serve Catherine the Great and had stayed on. It seemed clear from what he and others said that the presentation had gone well and arrangements were made for a smaller group to return to discuss it in more detail with those directly concerned.

Our next stop was Ekaterinburg, a thriving city in the middle of Russia, where bridal couples are photographed with one foot in Europe and the other in Asia. In 1941 trainloads of plant and machinery were transported from St Petersburg to Ekaterinburg, along with many treasures from the Hermitage, to save them from the Germans and the city was now an industrial centre of national importance. Known as Sverdlovsk in Soviet times, it reverted to its Tsarist name in 1992 in recognition of the fact that it was here that Tsar Nicholas II and his family were murdered. On this, my first visit to the city, I had no idea what the present generation of Russians felt about Tsardom and its end. I was taken to the site of the house where the murders were committed (the house itself having been demolished some years previously) and found that it was marked by a simple wooden cross with photographs of the family at its foot. Seeing this so soon after the end of Communist rule was a moving experience. It was a strange train of events which had brought me there at this particular time from my home in Kent, where one of my near neighbours is Princess Olga Romanoff whose father, Prince Andrew, was Tsar Nicholas's nephew.

Before I joined the consortium my colleagues had established cordial relations with the Governor of Sverdlovsk, who had visited London to raise awareness of the Urals region and the newly renamed Ekaterinburg (which had been a closed city for over fifty years) and had enlisted the co-operation of the Moscow Narodny Bank in London. He arranged for us to stay in a very comfortable state guesthouse reserved for VIPs. This hospitality was extended to us on all my visits to Ekaterinburg – no doubt because the hidden microphones installed in Soviet times were still in place and might be useful. Old habits die hard.

On this occasion the Governor was away and I was able to spend time visiting the office and meeting the three Russian members of the consortium's staff. Whoever recruited them had done an excellent job. The two senior members of the team were Yuri Semenov and Helen Vassina. Yuri was a medical doctor and former head of the regional health administration and, as well as being experienced and able, was one of the nicest human beings I have ever met. Helen, KGB-trained and with all the virtues and none of the vices of that august institution, liaised with the regional authorities, arranged our programmes and ran the office with great competence and skill; she also provided the non-Russian speakers among us with top quality interpretation. (The only one of us who spoke Russian really well was John Hardie, a cheerful former naval officer who learned it at the British government's expense during the Cold War. I used to ask John to propose a toast in Russian at some of the many banquets we attended; he used an old naval formula 'To our wives and sweethearts: may they never meet' which the male Russians always enjoyed.) The third member of the team was Irina Voronina who provided expert backing to Yuri and Helen with efficiency and charm.

All three coped remarkably with the strange business practices and requirements of their British visitors, which must have been something of a culture shock for people who had gained all their previous experience in the Soviet Union. For me, one happy consequence of my work with the consortium was that, after its dissolution, Helen Vassina and our German banker Klaus Doring got married; they now divide their time between Potsdam and Berkshire and I have formed a lasting friendship with them both.

The Russian staff were not the only ones to suffer a culture shock. The rest of us had a reasonable knowledge of Russia and its history but the Russia we knew was the Soviet Union, which was already two years old when I was born. Under the old regime, with all its faults, economic conditions and life generally were very predictable: but since Gorbachev's first visit to London the pace of change had been bewilderingly fast. On his appointment as General Secretary he had launched a programme of political and economic reform which led in 1989 to a democratically elected Parliament and the beginnings of a market economy; in 1990 to the abolition of the Communist Party's monopoly of power; and in 1991 to the dissolution of the Soviet Union.

When the Berlin Wall came down in 1989, Gorbachev made it clear that it was up to the peoples of Eastern Europe to decide what political system they wanted and that Moscow would not use military intervention to influence their choice. This was a historic decision for which, as was affirmed by his Nobel Peace Prize, Gorbachev deserves the world's gratitude and respect. He was, however, a product of the system under which he grew up and I thought at the time – and on the whole I still think – that the maverick Boris Yeltsin, who famously tore up his Communist Party card during a speech to the Russian Parliament, was a more suitable figure to lead Russia into the post-Communist world. On balance, it seemed to me that if Russia was to move successfully from the deeply entrenched but discredited system with which it had lived for seventy years to the totally different system in force in the rest of the developed world, it would need to make a complete break rather than a gradual transition.

The complete break favoured by Yeltsin was implemented by Yegor Gaidar, a 35-year-old economist who was in charge of the programme of economic reform introduced in 1990 and became acting Prime Minister in 1992. Gaidar, who was advised by the Harvard economist Jeffery Sachs and had the support of the World Bank and IMF, believed that to bring a market economy into being successfully, Russia needed to apply 'shock therapy', notably through privatisation and the abolition of price control and subsidies. This programme was very controversial and opinion on it in Russia was sharply divided.

The view of many, perhaps most, Russians was expressed by Irina Lobatcheva in her book *Russia in the 1990s*:[64]

64 Published in 2013 by Parallel Worlds' Books

> In the 1960s–1980s Soviet society provided the majority of Russians with a decent life, free from fear of unemployment, with plenty of opportunities for self-fulfilment and career advancement. Everyone had a right to a month's vacation and medical care was free, as well as education; even day-care cost next to nothing … The adoption of 'more advanced' free market and democratic principles of governing resulted in a drastic impoverishment of the majority of people … and we, ordinary Russians, enthusiastically participated in the peaceful demolition of the world superpower into a poverty-stricken country.

A different view was expressed by a supporter of Gaidar's shock therapy, Andrei Ostalski, who told the BBC:

> There were only two solutions – either introduce martial law and severe rationing or radically liberalise the economy. The first option meant going all the way back to the Stalinist system of mass repression. The second meant a colossal change – or rather a race – through uncharted waters with an unpredictable outcome.

In the consortium we were very conscious that the waters we were sailing through were indeed uncharted – people were making up the rules as they went along. The shock therapy which, for good or ill, Gaidar and his Western advisers favoured, created new opportunities for the smart, the adventurous, the well-connected and the corrupt to make money on a very large scale – hence the emergence in short order of the oligarchs. To begin with, the number of people who had the knowledge and ability to take advantage of these opportunities was small, but as news spread of the rich pickings to be had, more and more Russians looked for ways in which they too could benefit from the market economy, even if on a much smaller scale than the oligarchs.

The consortium had come equipped, through its association with the London branch of Moscow Narodny Bank, to set up arrangements for barter and various forms of counter-trading which would allow regional administrations to access the foreign exchange they would need to buy our products and services. A number of such arrangements were indeed made, though not on quite so large a scale as we had expected. It gradually became clear to us, however, that the financial arrangements in which most of our potential customers were interested were closer to home.

This was borne in on me through one episode in which the recollection of my own naivety still makes me blush. We made a practice of inviting Russians whom we considered serious prospects to visit us in Britain and see the factories where our products were made and the hospitals or other places where they were used. On one occasion we invited the medical authority of a particular city to send a team to the UK for a visit of this kind for which we would meet the delegation's foreign exchange expenses, as we usually did. I had met – and liked – the leader of the delegation, who treated me with true Russian hospitality when I visited him, so I returned the compliment by inviting him and his wife to come to our country home during the weekend before the London meetings began. I, of course, thought that this courtesy would enable us to get to know one another better and could generate a useful feeling of trust between us. He, though I think pleased by the invitation, clearly inferred from it that I had other, more private matters in mind for discussion between the two of us, in a secluded location with no hidden microphones. This kind of misunderstanding reflected a problem of different cultures of which we became more aware as time went on and was, I think, one of the main reasons why we were unable to achieve as much as we had hoped for.

After the initial visit to Ufa and Ekaterinburg (which I returned to several times) I took consortium teams to Perm, a rather drab city on the European side of the Urals where Dostoyevsky spent some years of exile in the 1850s, and to Tuymen, an attractive town on the western edge of Siberia with modern apartment blocks built in the 1940s by German prisoners of war. Building on Amersham's relationship with the Russian nuclear industry, Bruce Beharrel took a team to Chelyabinsk; and David Evans, who had joined as general manager of the BHCC after my appointment, took one to Togliatti, a centre of car manufacture on the Volga named after the founding Secretary of the Italian Communist Party. A visit to Irkutsk, deep in Siberia on the shores of Lake Baikal (the largest expanse of inland water in the world) was also planned. I had a great desire to visit Irkutsk, 'the Paris of Siberia', which the aristocratic Decembrist exiles of 1824 (and later their loyal wives who followed them into exile) turned into a thriving cultural centre, with an opera house and concert hall, but for some reason the visit never took place.

We invited delegations from all these cities to visit us in London, where I regularly hosted lunch or dinner for them at the Royal Thames Yacht Club in Knightsbridge, with a handsome silver bowl donated to the club by Tsar Nicholas in 1908 decorating the centre of the table. Relations with the authorities of these cities were always cordial and the visits which they and numerous doctors and other health-care staff paid to British hospitals under our auspices were, I believe, greatly appreciated. In our publicity material we said that 'the long-term vision of the consortium is to help the ordinary people of the former Soviet Union to enjoy the standard of healthcare that their counterparts in the West take for granted' and I like to think that through these programmes we made a worthwhile contribution to this.

In 1993 the Secretary of State for Health Virginia Bottomley (now Baroness Bottomley of Nettlestone) led a seventeen-man mission, of whom ten, including myself, were from the consortium, to Kazakhstan. This central

Asian country, though closely allied to Russia, had become an independent sovereign state on the break-up of the Soviet Union, with Nursultan Nazarbayev (the previous General Secretary of the local Communist Party) as its President. Mr Nazarbayev, to whom Tony Blair became adviser on good governance in 2011, was re-elected President in that year by a majority of 95.5 per cent and at the time of writing remains in office. Kazakhstan is largely a desert country but its principal city, Almaty, where we held our meetings, is a green place surrounded by apple orchards, nestling under the foothills of the Himalayas. In April, when we visited, the blossom was in full bloom and it was a delightful place to be. Fortunately, we were not allowed to visit Semipalatinsk, the desert area in the north of the country where between 1949 and 1991 the Russians tested their nuclear devices – though arguably a visit by a healthcare team would not have been a bad idea.

The Secretary of State and her delegation were hospitably received by the Kazakh government. My chief recollection is that, as the senior male member of the delegation, I was given the sheep's eyes to eat at the opening banquet – an experience which I am not in a hurry to repeat. The meetings were polite but formal and led nowhere. The Kazakh business culture was opaque and we did not have the key to access it. But Virginia Bottomley was, as she said at our meeting with the President, the first British Cabinet minister to set foot in the country and the visit was an interesting experience for us all.

In the early 1990s – notably by his handling of the attempted coup against Gorbachev by conservative hard-liners in August 1991 – Boris Yeltsin showed decisive leadership which served his country well. In 1992 he paid a successful visit to London, which passed off without any of the mishaps that afflicted his overseas trips in later years. Doreen and I attended a grand dinner hosted by John Major in the Painted Hall at Greenwich, where I had a short conversation with President Yeltsin and got ticked off for referring to Ekaterinburg by its old name of Sverdlovsk. Later he made a confident and visionary speech about 'Russia's progress along the road of democracy and reform towards a life worthy of a man, on which we will never turn back, however difficult it may be'.

There is, I think, no doubt that at this period Yeltsin reflected a widespread desire in Russia to make the reforms work. He received a firm vote of confidence in a referendum held the following year and for a while the prospects looked bright: but before long everything started to go pear-shaped. Converting the sclerotic command system of the latter day Soviet Union into a fully-fledged market economy was always going to be a herculean task and economic policy was not Yeltsin's forte. In retrospect it seems clear that the comprehensive programme of privatisation, which was at the heart of the strategy favoured by Gaidar and his Western advisers, was not well handled. The method chosen – and rushed through – gave too much scope for well-connected people who were interested only in making a fast buck to get hold of Russia's crown jewels (in the form of natural resources such as oil and metals); and the vast sums amassed by the oligarchs were an affront to the population at large at a time when the cost of daily living was rising steeply. The cause of reform, which the Russian masses had up to then broadly accepted, was hugely damaged by this and the general mood became one of 'every man for himself', in which there were bound to be more losers than winners.

Relations between the President and Parliament deteriorated sharply in 1993. Towards the end of the year Yeltsin tried to dissolve Parliament but the members refused to budge and in the constitutional crisis which followed Yeltsin brought in the army to enforce his policy. This led to ten days of fighting in the streets of Moscow which were said to be the worst since 1917 and cast a shadow over the rest of his Presidency. From then on the Russian economy grew steadily more chaotic, trading conditions (especially for non-resident companies) rapidly deteriorated and corruption flourished.

In its first two or three years the consortium made good progress. There was at that time an acute shortage of pharmaceuticals in Russia. Our first significant contract was to supply a portfolio of high quality pharmaceutical products to the Health Authority in Ekaterinburg. We later designed and supervised the construction of an oncology centre for the city, which I had the privilege of inaugurating with an appropriate plaque. In Perm we supplied a comprehensive range of medical products, including incubators and diagnostic drugs, for their mother and child centre and helped them to launch a regional programme of pre- and post-natal care. We also arranged for a significant number of health professionals and managers in the Urals region to receive training in NHS hospitals in the UK. In addition, we continued to search for new areas in which to promote the consortium's potential; Omsk and Nizhny Novgorod were soon added to the list and despite the founders' initial reservations we also took on some business in Moscow. We had always known that the consortium was a long-term venture in which the returns would not come quickly and for the time being the member companies were prepared to carry on in the hopes that market conditions would become more stable in the not too distant future.

Unfortunately, the constitutional crisis and the change of mood it precipitated took a heavy toll on Yeltsin, who despite his positive qualities, was *au fond* a deeply insecure man – he strongly reminded me of George Brown, the British politician for whom I had worked thirty years before. His consumption of vodka increased, his behaviour became more erratic and his health deteriorated, leading to a quadruple heart bypass in 1996. This greatly impaired his capacity to lead his country to better times and in 1997, as trading conditions in Russia showed no signs of improvement, we regretfully concluded that the time had come to wind up the consortium. Two years later Yeltsin resigned and handed over the Presidency to Vladimir Putin.

So ended my professional involvement with Russia – an extraordinary experience which, despite some disappointments, I found intensely rewarding. I had a great liking for Russia and its warm, stoical people, to whom history has dealt a poor hand. I wish them a better future.

It also brought to an end, at the age of seventy-eight, my working career.

–CHAPTER SEVENTEEN–

ENVOI

Any reader who has persevered thus far will realise that I have had a fortunate life. My parents, despite some problems in their own marriage – caused, I suspect, by the psychological impact on my father of his experiences in the First World War – brought me up in a secure and loving family environment that allowed me to grow into the optimistic and self-reliant person I became. I was given a privileged education at school and university which was as good as could be had anywhere in the world. Provided they survived the second war, young people of my generation – unlike their present day successors – had no difficulty in finding employment and could usually count on having a reasonable pension when they retired. This enabled me to have a varied and fulfilling career, which continued until I was nearly eighty, in exceptionally interesting times. As I have already mentioned, my marriage was the most important thing in my life and, together with the religious faith I acquired in middle age, has given it its meaning. It was a great sadness to us both that we had no children and this must, of course, have affected Doreen more deeply than me. But although it could have put a strain on our relationship, its effect was to bring us closer to one another – we were married for almost sixty years and did everything together. For all this and for the affection I have received over the years from family and friends I am grateful beyond words.

One important thing Doreen did for me was to introduce me to the world of painting. I came from a family whose great interests were music and books. It was through music that my parents met, at a country house concert where my mother was singing; they were both opera buffs and, true to the spirit of their generation, had a passion for Wagner which I fear I have never been able to share. My father's greatest interest was English (or rather, bearing in mind his love of Walter Scott and Robert Louis Stevenson, British) literature; he seemed never to be without a book in his hand, even when at the end of his life he had given up reading. But art played little part in their lives.

Doreen was musical – she was a good pianist and played the violin in an Essex orchestra – but her passion was for visual art of all kinds and in particular painting in oils, for which she herself had a natural gift. After leaving school she went to the University of Fribourg in Switzerland but, as war approached, she returned to England to study at Byam Shaw, a leading degree-level art school in London. For her, as for everyone else, the war changed everything. Her father, a naval officer who in World War Two served at sea until he was nearly sixty, wanted her to become a Wren but she decided to join the civil service instead. For some years she worked as a temporary Principal in Warwick Castle, which had been taken over by the Ministry of Supply for the duration, and in due course she moved to Whitehall. It was here that we met, having been separately invited to play tennis with two colleagues. The next day I wondered, for the first time in my thirty-year-old life, if I had at last met the woman I was going to marry – and I think that before long Doreen felt something similar. She enjoyed her work in the civil service and the companionship it brought and was good at both: but they – and later on, I fear, the demands of marriage – took up too much time to leave any over for serious painting and she was never able to realise her potential as an artist.

For this reason our association with the New English Art Club, under the Presidency of Ken Howard, Tom Coates, Jason Bowyer and Richard Pikesley in turn, has given us both particular pleasure over the years. The New English was set up in 1886 and its early membership included Whistler, Sargent, Sickert, Orpen and Augustus John. Its original purpose was to challenge the Royal Academy but it is now part of the artistic establishment and has a good claim to be the pre-eminent group of figurative painters at work in Britain today. Jane Bond, who painted the fine portrait of Doreen, included within the plate section of this book, is a longstanding member. The NEAC is also a very friendly, welcoming place and since Doreen died in 2009 I have given a major prize in her memory at its annual open exhibition in November. I have also been able to sponsor, in her name, the Drawing Room in the principal art museum in Canterbury, the recently refurbished Beaney House of Art and Knowledge.

A few years after we were married Doreen gave up her civil service career in order to support me in Delhi when, as described in Chapter 9, I was offered a post there. In this she was following the custom of the day, as my mother Chrissie had done in the previous generation. Chrissie was a highly talented soprano who left her Edinburgh home for a year's training in Paris when she was eighteen – a life-changing experience which nothing later quite matched. After her marriage to my father and the move south which followed it – and in her case too the disruption of a world war – she gave up any thoughts of a musical career in order to support him and bring up their two children. Once again I was a principal beneficiary – there is no doubt in my mind that my positive outlook on life and what George Brown called my 'laid-back confidence' owe a great deal to the full-time presence of a loving mother in my early childhood.

Looking back, I am very conscious that, despite their otherwise happy lives, there was an important part of both my wife and my mother which was unfulfilled because they had consciously subordinated their own aspirations and ambitions to the demands of their husbands' careers.

The same may have been true of my sister Mary. She was a highly intelligent woman with wide intellectual interests and a strong sense of social purpose who might well have gone into politics: but, having moved to Sheffield when her husband's first job took him there, gave up any idea of a full-time career after the war in order to raise her three daughters, whose affectionate company has given me so much happiness in recent years. All this – and perhaps my early experience of having a well-respected woman as my boss in Whitehall – has made me strongly supportive of the contemporary arguments in favour of rethinking women's role in society.

Times have, of course, greatly changed since then: but the problem of finding the right balance between the conflicting demands of marriage, parenthood and career still remains and seems in some ways to have become more acute. To my mind, the world (including not least my own Roman Catholic Church) has been exaggeratedly male-centred for far too long and the time has come for men to face up to this and make a deliberate effort to redress the balance. The current generation of young fathers seem to be making a better fist of things than their predecessors: but even in this country – let alone in so many other parts of the world – there is a long way to go before men and women are treated as genuine equals in society, with the same right to have their own needs and aspirations taken fully into account.

As a childless male I hesitate to suggest how this might be achieved. It seems to me that a good – and I think practicable – start might be to double the number of women in both Houses of Parliament within the next ten years. But it is really up to ordinary male citizens to bring about the required change in attitudes by their own behaviour and initiative. I hope that the coming generation will do better in this than mine has done.

APPENDIX I

Review of June Morris's *The Life and Times of Thomas Balogh: a Macaw Among Mandarins* (Sussex Academic Press, 2007) by Ronnie McIntosh

Balliol College Record, 1938

THE BALLIOL SCR has had its share of eccentrics over the years but Thomas Balogh, about whom June Morris has written a perspective and engaging book, was certainly one of its more exotic twentieth-century denizens.

Tommy (as we always called him) was a Hungarian economist, with the intellectual brilliance often found in that clever, complex race and a gift for provoking controversy. Though he retained his foreign accent and mannerisms all his life, he spent many years close to the heart of the political establishment of his adopted country and ended up as a working member of the House of Lords.

Morris, who knew him well in his later years and has interviewed an impressive list of Balliol men and others for her book, brings out vividly the conflicting responses evoked by Balogh's idiosyncratic personality. To many of those with whom he came in contact he appeared an opinionated and abrasive intriguer with a tendency to question the integrity of anyone who disagreed with him. To others – and especially his former pupils, of whom I am one – he was someone whose wide ranging intellect, original mind and irreverent sense of humour ensured that his company was never dull and often scintillating. By all accounts, not least his own, these qualities also made him attractive to a wide range of women friends. (When Tommy was made a minister at the Department of Energy in 1974 he told me with some satisfaction that at 68 he was the oldest man ever to achieve ministerial office for the first time – and in answer to my question he attributed his continuing vitality to 'aggression and sex'.)

I first encountered Balogh in 1946, not long after his election as a Fellow of Balliol, when I resumed my undergraduate career after six years of war and decided to switch from Greats to PPE. In the first few tutorials I was a bit put out to find that as I read my carefully prepared – and doubtless pedestrian – essays to him, Tommy would without warning stretch out on the floor and telephone his political friends in Hampstead. The third time this happened we had a sharp discussion about the correct etiquette for tutorials at English universities, after which Tommy gave up the telephone (though not the floor) and paid attention to the matter in hand. As a result I quickly discovered that the best I have ever encountered – and Morris confirms that this view was shared by practically all his former pupils whom she interviewed.

What impressed me most – and set him apart from such distinguished contemporaries as James Meade and J. R. Hicks – was his dismissive attitude towards economic theory and his conviction that political economy is best understood through careful study of actual, historical events (a conviction shared in a later generation by Alan Greenspan). Tommy's view was, I think, that the study of economics has value only as an aid to better political decision-making and that academically it should be regarded as a branch of history or politics rather than an intellectual discipline in its own right. When, for example, the subject for the next tutorial was to be exchange rate policy, he would not ask one to read any of the theoretical literature but to immerse oneself in the events leading up to Churchill's decision to return to the Gold Standard in 1925 and the consequences which flowed from this. His subsequent comments on these events illuminated the subject in a way in which – for me at least – no amount of theoretical analysis could have done and provided insights which I have found relevant all my life.

Tommy's association with Balliol was one of the two most important factors in his working life – the other being his friendship with Harold Wilson. Some years after his arrival in England Balogh came to the notice of Sandy Lindsay, an accomplished talent spotter whose support, as Master, was crucial to his election as a Fellow of Balliol, at the second attempt, in 1945. (According to Morris, rumour had it that his first attempt in 1943 was blocked by the Bank of England;

my guess is that this originated with Tommy himself, who would have considered it a more elegant explanation for his failure to get elected than what Morris thinks may have been the real reason – that a puritanical SCR turned him down on the grounds of his sexual indiscretions.) Whatever the truth may be, there is no doubt that Tommy was overjoyed to get the Fellowship and retained his loyalty and affection for the college to the end of his life.

His friendship with Harold Wilson had, of course, a seminal importance for Balogh's career. When they met in Oxford in 1938, Wilson was a 21-year-old economics tutor in his first job. Balogh was eleven years older and had accumulated a fair degree of experience in banking at home and abroad. The two men developed a close friendship to which the difference in age may have given some of the flavour of tutor-pupil relationship. Over the years, with Wilson's rise to the leadership of the Labour Party and then to Downing Street, the balance within the friendship inevitably shifted. But the easy companionship the pair had enjoyed in the early years remained; and although as Prime Minister he did not always accept Tommy's advice, I am not aware (having known them both well) that Harold Wilson ever seriously lost patience with his old friend, exasperating though the latter could be. Their long friendship was a genuine one, founded on mutual loyalty and respect, and was important to them both.

Morris writes well about their relationship during Tommy's years as the Prime Minister's economic adviser and gives one of the more balanced accounts of life in Downing Street at the time to appear in the growing literature on the subject. She devotes a good deal of space to Balogh's vendetta against the Whitehall mandarins. This proved largely counter-productive because his apparent paranoia on the subject and the extravagant terms in which he expressed his criticisms made it easy for his intended victims to deflect them.

Balogh was certainly wrong in supposing that most civil servants wanted to frustrate the Labour government's legitimate plans; on the contrary, the younger mandarins were disillusioned by the Tories' loss of direction during their long period in office and very ready to help the new government to try out its ideas. But Tommy's attacks on the 'gifted amateur' culture of the top civil servants and the general lack of professionalism in Whitehall were not so wide of the mark.

The triumvirate who ruled Whitehall during this period were not an impressive group. The Cabinet Secretary, Burke Trend, who was the particular target of Tommy's venom, was a strange, secretive man with whom few found it easy to work. Of the two joint permanent secretaries of the Treasury, one was described by Roy Jenkins in an interview for this book as 'a thoroughly third rate man' and the other showed unmistakable signs of mental instability during Edward Heath's confrontation with the miners in 1973. There was a widespread view in the 1960s that the civil service was not self-evidently fit for purpose and Wilson's decision to set up an enquiry into the recruitment and training of civil servants, under John Fulton (sometime fellow of Balliol – where else?), was generally welcomed. Balogh's criticisms of Whitehall, though intemperately expressed, were not without foundation.

However, Tommy's job was not to feud with civil servants (with whom, having worked in Whitehall during the war, Harold Wilson was generally comfortable) but to give advice on economic policy. The big question which confronted the Labour government on taking office in 1964 was whether to devalue the pound, on which an immediate decision was required. At the time the *bien pensants* in and around government, including virtually all the professional economists, favoured devaluation. Baolgh was the odd man out and, in intensive discussions which took place in the new government's first few days, he argued firmly against it – probably because he knew that Wilson had already decided it would be a political disaster for Labour and had accordingly ruled it out.

Balogh believed that one of the government's priorities should be to secure the trade union's agreement to a comprehensive prices and incomes policy. According to Morris, he had advocated this approach since the early 1940s as the essential underpinning of the full employment which all political parties were committed to aim for after the war. By 1964 it had secured quite widespread and, to a degree, bipartisan support; and the desirability of a formal incomes policy, enshrined in some joint declaration by government and unions and if necessary backed by legislation, had become part of the accepted establishment wisdom.

Thus began a strange interlude of fifteen years in which such previously unknown concepts as pay codes, norms, pauses and freezes became part of the ordinary currency of politics, as George Brown's tripartite Declaration of Intent in 1965 was followed by Ted Heath's statutory pay controls in 1972 and Jack Jones's Social Contact in 1975. In the event the unions proved unwilling or unable to enforce the degree of restraint in wage bargaining required to make this approach a success and incomes policy steadily unravelled over the years until it died an unlamented death in the 'winter of discontent' in 1978. Balogh watched this process unfold with dismay but not surprise, as the unions had clearly signalled what they thought of government intervention in their affairs by rejecting Barbara Castle's 'In Place of Strife' in 1969. He was convinced at the time that this would seal the fate of the incomes policy he had worked so hard to bring into being; and so it proved.

Towards the end of his life Tommy told Morris that he was disappointed that he had not been able to do more to influence events in the years he spent at the centre. There is no doubt that his abrasive temperament and impatience with the convoluted inefficiencies of government decision-making prevented him from taking advantage of his privileged access to Cabinet committees to build support for policies he favoured. But he was first and foremost a personal adviser to the Prime Minister, who looked to him to give advice which had not already been pre-digested in Whitehall committees and provided a difference slant from the recommendations he received from more conventional sources. Balogh's success in this was confirmed by a remark of Wilson's with which any adviser could be content: 'The things I get from Tommy are exaggerated but they always contain the kernel of what I want.' Balogh was, however, a man of his time and the causes he espoused – economic planning, intervention in industry and incomes policy – are no longer considered by many to be serious policy options.

During all his time in government, at first in Downing Street and later in the Energy Department, Tommy played an active role in the development of policy on North Sea oil. His overriding aim was always to maximise the benefits accruing to the national economy from this new resource and to prevent the international oil companies from creaming off more than their due share of the wealth extracted from below the seabed. I am not qualified to pass judgement on his activities in this field, but from what I know, I would guess that an expert verdict would be positive and that Tommy could legitimately take some credit for the favourable economic situation which later underpinned the Thatcher governments of the 1980s. Whether this would have pleased him is another question.

Aside from these weighty issues of national policy, it is clear from my own and others' experience, that Tommy was a gifted teacher whose insights illuminated parts which other tutors couldn't reach. He was also a man who, though he made a lot of enemies, enjoyed the respect and friendship – and often the affection – of many talented people in public and academic life. He was a many-sided man and this book does him full justice.

APPENDIX II

Extract from P. M. Heaton's *The South American Saint Line: History of a Welsh Shipping Venture* (The Starling Press Ltd., 1985)

THE SECOND CASUALTY occurred on November 28, of that same year, when the two-year-old pride of the fleet *St. Elwyn*, while on passage from Hull to Santos with a cargo of coal, was torpedoed and sunk by the German submarine *U130* about 500 miles East of Bishop Rock. Tragically twenty-nine members of her crew of forty were lost, the survivors being rescued by another Cardiff ship, Reardon Smith Line's *Leeds City* on December 3. Mr. R. H. Davis, a Cadet, wrote an account of the loss of the *St. Elwyn* which appeared in *Reef Knot*, the house magazine of The South American Saint Line. It is reproduced in full.

At the time she was lost the *St. Elwyn* was the Flagship of the Saint Line Fleet.

She made her first voyage in November, 1938 and was an improvement on the previous Saint vessels built by Messrs. J. L. Thompson and Sons Ltd., Sunderland, and engined by Messrs. Whites Marine Engineering Co. Ltd., – she was a very comfortable and happy ship.

Early in November, 1940, we sailed from Hull with a cargo of coal for Santos, commanded by Captain Daniels, D.S.C. We proceeded up the North East Coast to Methil and after a short stay, sailed as Commodore vessel in a North-about coastal convoy to Oban situated on the West coast of Scotland; the voyage had been uneventful so far. Here the Ocean-going convoy was assembled and we finally weighed anchor and proceeded on our way.

It was not long before we ran into a South-Westerly gale and difficulty was found in keeping station. One night there was a very heavy rainstorm, the weather deteriorating, and at dawn the following morning we saw that the two outer columns of the convoy had drifted away from the main convoy. However, we continued on our way with one destroyer as escort.

When about 500 miles out from the U.K. the convoy dispersed, as was the practice in those days, and we immediately set a Southerly course for Santos.

Gun watches had been kept by two Naval Gunners and members of the crew but they had no occasion to be busy.

Our defence equipment consisted of a 4in. B.L. gun and a Mills bomb ejector at the stern, 1 Oerlikon on the Bridge and a kite which was flown from the foremast.

The weather was still 'dirty' and as I came out of my cabin a sea broke over the boat deck and bowled me along to an awning stanchion which knocked out my two front teeth. Those who know the *St. Elwyn* will realise how bad it was for seas to come aboard on that deck.

The day following the dispersal of our part of the convoy we met our fate.

The other Apprentice, John Richards, of Newport, and I were having a cup of cocoa contemplating an early turn-in after a tiring day when suddenly at 6.30 p.m. there was a terrific crash causing the ship to vibrate violently for a few seconds. The lights failed and as we groped for our life-saving waistcoats we heard the lifeboat stations signal sounded on the siren.

Coming out on deck, into the inky blackness, it was found that the torpedo had stuck us on the port side in the engine room and that the force of the explosion had wrecked the port lifeboat which was swung out. The Chief Engineer, Mr. Cuthbert Gould, endeavoured to go below but was unable to do so owing to a twisted mass of gratings and ladders.

All hands were now assembled on the boat deck and as the lowering of the starboard boat commenced, a second torpedo struck us in the after part port side, shooting hatches and coal into the air.

The vessel was rapidly settling down and seas were constantly breaking over us. The for'ard raft was cut adrift and it slid into the water; a few seconds later it was piled up on the bridge.

The for'ard fall of the starboard boat slipped as it was being slackened causing the bow of the lifeboat to cant and throw out the Carpenter who was tending the falls. At that moment the ship sank, nobody knows exactly what happened, and all I can remember is gripping stanchions and hand-rails, only to be torn away by the force of the water. It seemed to me as if I had swallowed gallons of water and there was a thunderous roar in my ears.

I eventually found myself on the surface of a much calmer sea which we found out later must have been the effect of the fuel oil.

I saw the lifeboat silhouetted against the sky and after a short swim managed to get my arms over the gunwale and was hauled inboard by the Carpenter and Apprentice John Richards.

We eventually helped others into the boat and finally totalled seventeen out of a crew of about thirty-eight and five passengers. We had a terrific struggle to get the 2nd Officer, Alan Brightwell, into the boat – he had his bridge coat on and this became very heavy as it was soaked.

We were all feeling exhausted but eventually pulled him in. The seventeen in the boat consisted of: Mr. L. Williams, Chief Officer; Mr. A. Brightwell, 2nd Officer; Mr. P. Thomas, 4th Engineer; The 2nd Radio Officer; The 3rd Radio Officer; R. H. Davis, Apprentice; J Richards, Apprentice; 'Putsch', Ship's Cook; The Carpenter; Tom Burrows, D. E. M. S. Gunner; Six A.B.'s and Firemen; one Passenger – an Austrian Refugee.

Everyone was seasick and no wonder considering the amount of sea-water and fuel oil we had swallowed and the totally different motion of a small boat.

It was decided to stay in that area all night in the hope of picking up more survivors, but unfortunately no one was seen; it was estimated that eight minutes elapsed from the time the torpedo struck to the sinking of the vessel; it was a miracle that seventeen reached the lifeboat.

The wind howled all that night and the spray felt like broken glass to our faces. We put the protective hood up for'ard but soon had to take it down as we were unable to keep the boat head to sea.

Our main worry now was lack of experience in boat work. However, we kept her on an even keel and survived that dreadful night.

A tanker was seen and we used two of our precious flares, but she proceeded on her way.

At the crack of dawn we took stock of ourselves; a sorry sight we must have looked. Hair matted with fuel oil, cold and wet. We were about 500 miles off Northern Ireland but we had a good stock of Provisions – Biscuits, Tinned Milk, Tinned Sausages, Tinned Tomatoes and Corned Beef, two barracas of Water, two bottles of Brandy and a quantity of cigarettes, also half a dozen blankets; these had become wet and did not afford much warmth.

The sail was in good condition but our personal clothing was not. Most of us had a singlet, trousers and jacket, hardly suitable for Winter in the North Atlantic.

There was a Westerly wind and we set an Easterly course for Ireland. The wind was fresh and we made good progress. Each man took an hour trick at the helm and the others took spells at bailing as the boat was damaged on the port bow and a leak developed, also an occasional sea lopped aboard.

Food and water were rationed out at dawn, midday and dusk. The dusk issue being followed by a small tot of brandy to help keep us warm. The fifty cigarettes did not last long but they were a great help, as were the tinned tomatoes which were very good for quenching the thirst.

Another vessel was sighted during the early morning of the second day and we used our remaining flares but were unable to attract her attention.

The Third Radio Officer had not been too well and seemed to be suffering from shock. He also had a very nasty wound to his back.

It was his first trip and this last incident seemed to discourage him further. We all tried to help and cheer him but it was to no avail. The next morning we were unable to awaken him and apparently he had passed away quietly during the night.

The carpenter wrapped the body in a blanket which was then sewn up and weighed with a grappling iron. About 10.00 a.m. the sail was lowered and as we wallowed in the swell all hands stood up and sang 'Abide with me' and the body was slipped silently into the sea.

We immediately hoisted sail again to get under way. Nobody spoke for a long time. I think our thoughts were of home and our people and whether we would be able to stick it.

The wind was still fresh Westerly and very often became so strong that we had to lower the sail. Spray was constantly drenching us with the wind; we were all very cold.

Our feet and hands were beginning to show signs of swelling on the fourth day and we paired off to massage each other.

We lowered the sail during the night as we heard the sound of diesel motors; this was assumed to be a 'U' boat on the surface and there was a distinct smell of fuel oil. We all kept very silent and we breathed again as the sound passed away.

Good progress was made during the next day and night. It became very cold that night, the wind veered to N.W. and those who had the helmsmen's job had found their hands and arms like blocks of ice after about fifteen minutes.

About midnight on 3/4 December another ship was sighted; she was quite close to us and the difficultly was to attract her attention. We could see her silhouette plainly after about ten minutes. All hands started to shout their heads off and our only light – the oil lamp in the lifeboat compass was held up. Not a bright light by any means. However we were thankful that they had seen it and were very grateful for the excellent look-out that the ship was keeping. There was just one short flash from the torch on the bridge to acknowledge our cries. She stopped her engines and swung towards us, while we had lowered the sail and got the oars out.

Rowing was a very painful business and after what seemed an age we were near enough to take their heaving lines. We eventually got alongside but there was a heavy swell running. One moment we were level with the deck and the next under the keel. They had a rope ladder over the side and it was quite a feat to get on to it as we were not too strong by this time.

When my turn came I got halfway up, lost my grip, and crashed back into the water between the lifeboat and the ship's side. With the ranging of the lifeboat I thought I would fracture all my ribs, but I wasn't there long enough for that to happen. Quick as a flash the Bosun of the ship jumped from the deck onto the lifeboat mast and shinned down it, hauling me inboard. I then went up with a heaving line around.

We were all taken along to the saloon to get things sorted.

We learned that we were on board the S.S. *Leeds City*, commanded by Captain Ward and owned by the Reardon Smith Line. Everything was done to make us comfortable. Our boots and shoes had to be cut off and our various cuts and abrasions dressed. The Officers and crew gave up their bunks to us and we looked forward to a long deep sleep. However, this was impossible owing to the extreme pain of the returning circulation.

On the 6 December, the *Leeds City* anchored in the Clyde. An ambulance launch came out to take us ashore, and on the shore ambulances were waiting to whisk us off to the Smithson Casualty Hospital, Greenock, where we arrived at 6 p.m.

Here the nurses were kindness itself and we were grateful for all they did for us. Alan Brightwell was in the worst condition and very nearly lost his feet, but he made good progress and recovered. Unfortunately he lost his life later through Smallpox while serving on the M.V. *St. Essylt.*

Our first visitor next morning was none other than Captain W. Rees, who brought with him some very welcome cigarettes, writing paper, envelopes and stamps. It was a very good sight to see him.

Finally, one by one, we were discharged from hospital and went our various ways. I was the last to leave Scotland, after four months at Smithson Hospital I was transferred to Ballochmyle Hospital, Ayrshire, for the amputation of the tops of my fingers and eventually arrived home in August, 1941.

APPENDIX III

YACHTING PERSONALITIES

***Scottish Yachtsman*, 1952**

It is difficult to realise, when one sees the tall, straight figure of Mr. A. W. Steven walking down the jetty at Hunter's Quay and rowing himself out to *Jenetta* in his dinghy, that he went for his first sail as long ago as 1868. In the period during which he has been sailing the whole development of yachting, from the haphazard affair of a sail stuck in a boat to the highly scientific business that it is now, has taken place; the development from the *Comet* owned by his father, to the 12 Metre of which he is the owner now. During that period yachting on the Clyde, too, has gone through many changes and the tide has flowed and ebbed in number and popularity. It swept up to its great, fashionable, exciting climax in the late '90s and has returned again to the more modest, humdrum present day, reminiscent of those days of

Sketch by Ronald Barge

that first sail over eighty years ago. But if Mr. Steven wished to add his record, if it were not unique enough on his own account, he could say that his father became a well known member of the sailing community in the 1850s and took part in the first regatta of the Clyde Model Yacht Club, not the Royal Clyde, and was a Flag Officer of the Royal Northern Yacht Club between 1880 and 1892.

But Mr. Steven was not really greatly interested in what was going on during his first sail in 1868, for he was very young. His first race was in a yacht belonging to Mr. Peter Donaldson, of a shape which would horrify most of us to-day, a 42 ft. overall, 27 ft. on the waterline, with a beam of 4 ft. 6 in., all surmounted by a cloud of canvas, the area of which was unmeasured and forgotten; and it was not until he had left Merchiston that he begin to make himself felt as a person to be reckoned with in Clyde yachting.

Although at that time there was a fleet of very large yachts of all sorts and shapes in which anything less than 40 tons was regarded as small, and although we may regard that as the principal significance of that period of yachting – there was a hard core of youngsters racing and building small boats. These boats for many years were the training ships of the keen and likely steersmen to come and are now, still, in many instances, sailing up the West Coast every summer under the burgee of a member of the Clyde Cruising Club.

The young Steven started racing in his brother's boat in the 17/19 Class in a yacht which he shared with him, the *Asthore*, his first boat being *Rosalind*, in the same Class. This was a Class which kept its popularity for over eight years, until all the great designers had had a hand in designing a boat for it. The Class was finally burst by *Hatasoo*, which won practically all the prizes in 1896 – but she was a racing machine and the limit of development in the Class. They were, in modern eyes and in fact, over-canvassed, but Mr. Steven maintains that they would stand up with any modern yacht if for no other reason than that they lay over so far that they offered hardly any resistance to the breeze.

His *Nirvana* is lying, one is entitled to suppose, to this very day at the bottom of the chain at Barnhilt Buoy. He was racing in the 17/19 Class, running in a strong wind towards Barnhilt Buoy, round which they had to gybe. *Nirvana*, Mr Steven's boat, had the inside position and *Fricka* gybed too soon, took charge and rammed *Nirvana* amidships, striking her with her bowsprit below the water-line. The end of her bowsprit broke off and she rammed it further into the side of *Nirvana*. There was a rough sea and the continued jabbing of the bowsprit end began to open up the hole in *Nirvana* until it was about two feet long by a foot high. The crew of the *Nirvana* very wisely crept on board *Fricka*, but the boats, being on opposite gybes, turned round and round each other again and again, until there was a new danger that *Nirvana* might pull *Fricka* down with her until she filled also. Mr. Steven went back on board *Nirvana*, pulled in the mainsheet and tied the tiller to windward, till at least they were able to break the two apart. Mr. Steven jumped on board *Fricka* and watched *Nirvana* make a very graceful and dignified exit to the bottom of the sea.

Professor Teacher, in his history of the 19/24s, gives to Mr. Steven the credit of having put forward the idea which started that remarkable class in 1897. It was built to a simple rule devised by Fife and G. L. Watson, which could, with advantage, be resurrected. Fife, Linton Hope, Peter McLean of Rosneath, who actually built the prototype, and Mylne, all designed boats of the Class in their year. Mylne's boat was the first racing boat which he ever laid down on the drawing board. A. W. Steven in *Verenia*, the Fife boat, was top of the Class, with 25 prizes to Mr. D. T. Morrison's 17 in *Trebor*, and Mr. Steven won the No. 2 Tarbert Cup as well.

But from the beginning of the century his business was making more demands upon his time and, until 1914, he sailed other people's boats when he was free and, let it be said, sailed them with considerable success. He sailed for many years in the 23 footer class, another very fine class, very fast for their length and very seaworthy. Even with the 750 square feet of canvas, they very seldom had to reef. In *Dora*, belonging to Mr. Ronald Barge, he made a record which I doubt has ever been equalled, by winning every race in the Clyde Fortnight, eleven races in all.

With the beginning of World War I sailing, of course, stopped, but he did not return to it after the War but waited for almost twenty-two years before he did so. It was a chance meeting with Mr. J. D. G. Hendry in Euston Station in 1935 which brought him back from his country pursuits of fishing and shooting and deer-stalking, to his old way in the sea. In partnership with 'Lordy' Hendry he purchased *Carol* and was amazed by the development of the Eight Metre Class since he had last seen them. In the early days of the century, and in the early days of the Metre Rule, they had been regarded as poor boats. The 23 footers could sail past them to windward at any time they chose, but it was a profoundly different vessel that he found when he returned to race in the famous *Carol*. The changing Metre Rule had by that time produced what was probably the finest racing boat afloat, the modern Eight Metre, and after World War II he returned to the Eight Metre Class in *Felma*, the last Fife Eight Metre, which he brought up to the Clyde from the South.

And now he has *Jenetta*, a Twelve Metre which is the headache of the Handicap Committee, as, despite a handicap, she always seems to win. But she is not used only as a racing machine. He sailed her last summer round Skye and has raced her every year in the Highland Regattas since they were started again after the War. Mr. Steven is Rear-Admiral of the Mudhook – but Flag Officers' appointments are not new to him, for in 1895 he was Commodore of the Clyde Sailing Club.

He has brought into our modern sailing world much of the graciousness and dignity of the period during which he learned his sailing and we hope that these qualities, so rare in our modern world, will long be with us.

APPENDIX IV

TREASURY'S PRICES AND INCOMES MAN

'Men and Matters' column, *Financial Times*, 11 December 1972

WITH THE APPOINTMENT of Ronald McIntosh as deputy secretary in charge of co-ordinating pay and prices policy, the Treasury seems to be extending its grip over another key area of economic policy. The £10,500-a-year job was formerly part of a much wider Treasury brief over the budget and economic policy. Now this has been divided up and incomes and prices policy – until now directed by McIntosh over at the Department of Employment – elevated to separate status.

McIntosh, 53, is not a Treasury man, but he has always been an 'economic' civil servant building up, over the years, a wide knowledge of industrial affairs and regional policies. He first attracted notice when he worked on regional problems in the North East in the later years of the Macmillan government. This was followed up by a spell as under-secretary at the Board of Trade during Mr. Heath's term there (he shares the Prime Minister's love of sailing), and four years at the Department of Economic Affairs working on industrial policy.

The last two years have taken him to the Department of Employment and into the thick of the wages battle. He was in charge of the policy of de-escalating claims in the public sector which worked until the miners' strike and then collapsed. During the 'N minus 1' phase he was the principal civil servant going round industry trying to persuade employers not to give in to heavy wage claims.

McIntosh's career has given him the kind of experience of the world outside Whitehall which the Permanent Secretary at the Treasury, Sir Douglas Allen, has said he wants in the department. He also takes with him a reputation for openness and sociability. It remains to be seen whether he can withstand the Treasury's ability to remodel newcomers in its own image.

INDEX